He Walks with Us

MARY L. LYON

Inspiring Voices®
A Service of Guideposts

Inspiring Voices books may be ordered through booksellers or by contacting:

Inspiring Voices
1663 Liberty Drive
Bloomington, IN 47403
www.inspiringvoices.com
1 (866) 697-5313

ISBN: 978-1-4624-0950-1 (sc)
ISBN: 978-1-4624-0951-8 (e)

Library of Congress Control Number: 2014907315

Printed in the United States of America.

Inspiring Voices rev. date: 04/30/2014

Dedication

Nancy L. Kearney
January 18, 1948 – April 1, 2014

We will be together again in heaven.
I love you and miss you.

Contents

Acknowledgement

THERE ARE SEVERAL PEOPLE WHO HELPED THIS DREAM OF MINE become a reality.

NK – You probably have the book memorized as many times as I read it to you. Thank you for patiently listening to me as I made my corrections.

NB – Our banter made the book better. Thank you reading and re-reading. You were an encouragement to me.

AJ – You have such a creative talent. Thank you for sharing your gift with me.

Inspiring Voices Publishing – Thank you for your assistance and guidance as I saw this dream fulfilled. You were very patient with this new author.

And finally, I thank Him who walks with me through His truths to bring me to this place. To Him be the glory.

Foreword

I have known Mary for 30 years. She used to babysit our five daughters. When she approached me and asked if I would mentor her, I said it would have to happen on the "go" as she engaged in our family life. Immediately her impeccable character showed up in the ways she gave sacrificially to serve our family. We became very close and our friendship has grown from there.

When she told me she wanted to write a book and told me the book she wanted to write, it didn't surprise me. She has always been passionate about her walk with God and deeply cares about people knowing and experiencing God's love for them. I believe it is a book that needed to be written.

What caught me by surprise is how quickly she wrote it. We would talk as she was writing and each day I would get another chapter. It was so clear that this was God's message he had placed on her heart and she felt compelled to share it with others. It wasn't hard for her to write it because the message flowed from her own experience of walking with Christ. As she shared the chapters with me, I realized these are the truths that have driven her life for so many years… powerful, powerful, life-changing truths.

She does not mince words, she tells it like it is. Her comment to me more than once was that she did not want to dilute the truth. She hoped to communicate clearly but not at the expense of God's word. God's word was paramount. It is His word that changes lives.

Our relationship with God is a walk. In all the years I have known Mary she has passionately pursued God as **she has walked with Him** day by day. However, as she has grown and matured in her understanding of who God is, she is realizing that the depth of their relationship comes from God pursuing her as **He walks with her** day by day. Mary was determined that walk would be in the title. As the title unfolded I caught her vision. It is His walk with us.

I encourage everyone to take the time to read *He Walks with Us*. Your own walk with God will be challenged but it is also a great resource for helping younger Christians as God begins to walk with them. I have already begun recommending this book to other friends and ministries.

May this book bless your walk with God causing you to grow in your intimacy with Him as He walks with you.

Nancy Butkowski
Campus Crusade for Christ Family Life Ministry (40 years)
Author/Speaker

Introduction

THE TITLE OF THIS BOOK IS HOW I EXPERIENCE THE CHRISTIAN life. God walks with me. He walks with me through the ups and downs of life. He is always there with me.

When I set out to write a book, I wanted to help others who struggle with the day to day challenges with living. I wanted to write a book about the Christian struggle. Well, once I started writing this is the book that poured out of my heart.

The truths that follow are the strength of His walk with me. These truths help me get through Romans 7 to Romans 8. They keep me grounded in God's commitment to me as my Father. My hope and prayer is that these truths will help you.

As I wrote this book, I was struck by the strength of the message of God's forgiveness. We are forgiven children of God. We have an eternal relationship with God the Father. It is a powerful message.

I believe in the relationship that we have with God in Christ. I believe I can come before God and call Him Daddy. I believe God is alive and well in my soul. I believe that God the Father takes me by the hand and walks with me.

I also believe that I am a sinner who presses on until the day I am with Him. Let me clarify, I am a forgiven sinner. As Christians, we are blessed beyond all other people because we have the forgiveness of God in Christ Jesus. Our specialness is His specialness in us.

I hope as you read the chapters that follow you will grow deeper in your love relationship with our God and experience anew Him walking with you. I say with the Apostle Paul, Ephesians 1:17-19:

> "that the God of our Lord Jesus Christ, the Father of glory; may give to you a spirit of wisdom and of revelation in the knowledge of Him. I pray that the eyes of your heart may be enlightened, so that you may know what is the hope of His calling, what are the riches of the glory of His inheritance in the saints, and what is the surpassing greatness of His power toward us who believe."

Chapter 1

He Walks With Us

The message of this book is about His walk with us. It is about God the Father taking us by the hand and walking with us. It is about God placing His truths in our hearts.

The truths I chose are the ones that have been critical in God's walk with me. These truths ground me in His love as my Father. These are His truths He uses as He walks with me through the ups and downs of life; truths that support my footsteps as God and I walk together.

I believe God walking with us started in the Garden of Eden. Genesis 3:8 tells us:

> "And they heard the sound of the Lord God walking in the garden…"

Adam and Eve heard God walking in the garden. With all the other animals walking about, Adam and Eve knew the sound of God walking in the garden. God had walked in the garden before. God had walked with Adam and Eve before.

Genesis 3:9 reads:

> "Then the Lord God called to the man, and said to him, "Where are you?"

God knew where man was but I think it is poignant that He asked. I believe it was customary for God to walk with Adam and Eve. God had come as usual but Adam was not waiting for Him. Adam was pre-occupied.

Adam's pre-occupation was his sin. He knew he was naked and so he hid from God. His guilt prevented him from freely walking with God. Our guilt can keep us from freely walking with God.

I believe in Christ that we have that wonderful intimacy of walking with God restored. God has come to the gardens of our lives to walk with us. God wants to walk with us. He wants to take us by the hand, as a father does his child, and walk with us. I let God the Father take me by the hand and walk with me (I actually sometimes squeeze my hand to give me that physical realization that God is holding it). It is a very secure place for my life.

A very striking image of God walking with His children is God's presence during the Israeli nation's wondering in the wilderness. We read of this wonderful testimony in Exodus 40:34-38:

> "Then the cloud covered the tent of the meeting, and the glory of the Lord filled the tabernacle. And Moses was not able to enter the tent of meeting because the cloud had settled on it, and the glory of the Lord filled the tabernacle. And throughout all their journeys whenever the cloud was taken up from over the tabernacle, the sons of Israel would set out; but if the cloud was not taken up, then they did not set out until the day when it was taken up. For throughout all their journeys, the cloud of the Lord was on the tabernacle by day, and there was fire in it by night, in the sight of all the house of Israel."

When we review the passage, God did not just walk with His people, He led His people. God decided when they set out and when they waited. God was the author of their journey.

God led them on the journey. God walked with them on the journey. All of Israel could see God leading them and walking with them. God waited with them on the journey. Every day the Israeli nation had a testimony that God was with them and walking with them.

We also have a daily testimony of God walking with us through Christ who is in our hearts. God leads us and walks with us in Christ. He does so through His Son, Jesus Christ, and through His Spirit who dwells within us. He is always with us.

The truths that follow guide my journey as He walks with me. God has used the journey through these truths to deepen His walk with me.

When we talk about our walks in Christ we need to be mindful that He indeed walks with us. He is the leader for the journey. He is in control of the journey. We are because God is. We could not walk in Christ apart from God working in us.

As we study these truths together, let's experience Him walking with us. Let's experience Him and His truths in a new way. Let's pray, Abba Father, please take me by the hand and walk with me.

Psalms 23 so beautifully illustrates God walking with us at all times. I have prayed this psalm during my darkest moments.

> "The Lord is my shepherd, I shall not want.
> He makes me lie down in green pastures;
> He leads me beside quiet waters.
> He restores my soul;
> He guides me in the paths of righteousness
> For His name's sake.
> Even though I walk through the valley of the shadow
> of death,

> I fear no evil; for Thou art with me:
> Thy rod and Thy staff, they comfort me.
> Thou dost prepare a table before me in the presence of my enemies;
> Thou hast anointed my head with oil;
> My cup overflows.
> Surely goodness and lovingkindness will follow me all the days of my life,
> And I will dwell in the house of the Lord forever.

God wants to walk with you! God wants to walk with me! God wants to walk with us!

Saving Faith

"What will a man be profited, if he gains the whole world, and forfeits his soul (Matthew 16:26)?"

Chapter 2

Introduction

When talking about God walking with us, it is essential that we have a saving faith in Christ. It is this relationship with Christ that is of concern. If you have not placed your faith in Christ, I hope the truth of a Saving Faith opens your heart to Christ. If you have placed your faith in Christ, I hope this truth strengthens your faith and helps you share your saving faith with others.

As in any relationship, there are a few things we learn about the individual and how they relate before we make a 'true' commitment to the relationship. Well, the same is true for us to make a commitment of saving faith in Christ and have a relationship with God the Father through Christ. There are a few fundamental Biblical truths that need to be known and believed.

In order to truly have a saving faith in Christ, in order for a Christian to truly have a relationship with God the Father, he/she needs to believe that God exists and He has spoken, sin exists, the penalty for sin exists, and Christ's finished work exists. An individual needs to understand that there is the problem of sin in one's relationship with God and saving faith in Christ is the only solution.

We are called Christians because in Christ we are partakers of His finished work. We have saving faith in Christ's finished work to heal our broken relationship with our God.

God walking with us does not make sense without understanding the relationship a believer has with God the Father through Jesus Christ. My goal is not to provide a theological debate concerning these spiritual truths, but to provide the reader an understanding of saving faith in Christ. Everything we have as Christians, we have because of Christ. It is in His finished work.

Chapter 3

God Exists and He Has Spoken

It astounds me that people can deny the existence of God. How can a person look at the world around him/her and not believe in God is beyond me. Now, people who do not believe in God feel the same way about me.

My first response to them, however, is that if God does not exist, I have not lost anything by believing. If God does exist, they have lost everything by not believing.

Creation begs belief in a Creator. We exist. An apologetic I like to use with doubters to explain the need for a God for our own existence is:

1. Something exists.
2. Something cannot come from nothing.
3. Therefore, for something to exist, something has to have already existed always.

For me, as a believer, that something that has always existed is the God of the Bible. I believe the Bible is the inerrant Word of God.

I believe in the God of the Bible. I believe God exists and that He has spoken through His written Word, the Bible, and through His living Word, Jesus Christ.

Being a Christian requires a belief in God and that He has spoken. The Book of John, Chapter 1 verses 1- 18 reads:

> "In the beginning was the Word, and the Word was with God, and the Word was God. He was in the beginning with God. All things came into being by Him, and apart from Him nothing came into being that has come into being. In Him, was life, and the life was the light of men...But as many as received Him, to them He gave the right to become children of God, even to those who believe in His name, who were born not of blood, nor of the will of the flesh, nor of the will of man, but of God. And the Word became flesh, and dwelt among us, and we beheld His glory, glory as of the only begotten from the Father, full of grace and truth... For of His fulness we have all received, and grace upon grace. For the law was given through Moses; grace and truth were realized through Jesus Christ. No man has seen God at any time; the only begotten God, who is in the bosom of the Father, He has explained Him."

One cannot have faith as a Christian apart from the word of God. God exists and He has spoken. He is His Word. A common expression use to be that a man was only as good as his word and the word of a good man was all you needed.

God is as good as His word. And His Word, Jesus Christ, is all we need to have a right relationship with our God; for God to walk with us.

I remember a sharing experience I had with a college student. Her comment was that because she did not know God, He could not exist. My comment to her was that a few moments ago she did not know me and yet I existed. I explained to her that her knowledge of me was not necessary for my existence.

I went on to point out that a lot of people in this world exist without her knowledge of them. None of us need her knowledge of us for our existence.

I further explained that God exists with or without her knowledge of Him. The bigger question was, "Does she want to know God?"

Do you want to know God?

Do you want God to walk with you?

Chapter 4

Existence of Sin

THE FIRST FEW CHAPTERS OF THE BOOK OF GENESIS TELL THE story of creation (yes, I believe the story) and the introduction of sin. In Genesis 2:17, God clearly tells Adam,

> "but from the tree of the knowledge of good and evil you shall not eat, for in the day that you eat from it you shall surely die."

Well, Adam and Eve ate the fruit from the tree of good and evil and Genesis 3:7 tells us

> "then the eyes of both of them were opened and they knew that they were naked; and they sewed fig leaves together and made themselves loin coverings."

After eating the fruit, Adam and Eve felt shame, which means they felt guilt about their actions - they were experiencing feelings resulting from their sin. What is sin? It is disobeying a command given by the Lord. Adam and Eve disobeyed by the eating of the fruit.

The disobedience started in their hearts. The eating was the action that followed the heart's desire for the fruit. Their hearts wanted what they wanted more than what God wanted. And thus, they sinned.

One consequence of the sin is that Adam and Eve can no longer be naked with one another. Sin against God impacted their relationship with one another.

A second consequence, and a more critical one, is that it impacted their relationship with God; continuing in Genesis 3:8,

> "And they heard the sound of the Lord God walking in the garden in the cool of the day, and the man and his wife hid themselves from the presence of the Lord God among the trees of the garden."

Adam and Eve hid from God. God walked with them and talked with them and now they are hiding. Their relationship with God was forever changed. Man's relationship with God was forever changed. There is now spiritual separation in the relationship between God and man.

Don't get too upset with Adam and Eve because we too are sinners and sin every day. And yes, I believe any one of us given the choice given Adam and Eve would have done the same thing and eaten of the fruit.

Romans 3:23 tells us,

> "for all have sinned and fall short of the glory of God."

It is very clear from this verse that we are all sinners and all fall short of the glory of God. It isn't just the vile among us, but all of us.

History is filled with the hateful sins of humanity. We are sinners. If you think you are perfect and without sin, just ask a few people who know you well and they will be able to point out your flaws.

Sin exists in our hearts.

Do you grasp that you are a sinner?

Chapter 5

Penalty for Sin

I WANT TO TAKE A LITTLE TIME HERE FOR REFLECTION. REMEMBER in Genesis 2:17 that God says in that day you shall surely die. However, Adam and Eve did not physically die. So, what happened?

What kind of dying was God predicting? I believe God was predicting a spiritual death; spiritual separation from God. They hid from God, they experienced a brokenness in their relationship with God. Adam and Eve died a spiritual death - they knew they were naked.

The penalty for sin is spiritual death. It is a spiritual brokenness in man's relationship with His Creator. We often think about our physical death, but I believe it's the spiritual death that is of significance. Man was created to have fellowship with his creator. When man sinned that fellowship was broken.

It is important that we reflect on the impact sin has on our relationship with God. We often sweep our little 'sins' under the rug as part of being human. And yes, it is part of being a sinful human. But those little sins keep us from enjoying fellowship with our God and do need to be addressed. Fortunately, as we will discuss in the next chapter, God provided a solution for our sins and the penalty for them.

Our physical death also is a result of the sin. Please read Genesis 3:22-24,

> "Then the Lord God said, "Behold, the man has become like one of Us, knowing good and evil; and now, lest he stretch out his hand, and take also from the tree of life, and eat, and live forever" - therefore the Lord God sent him out from the garden of Eden, to cultivate the ground from which he was taken. So He drove the man out; and at the east of the garden of Eden He stationed the cherubim, and the flaming sword which turned every direction, to guard the way to the tree of life."

I believe physical death was God having mercy on us from having to live in this body of sin for eternity. God guarded the way to the tree of life so man would not live forever in a state of sin.

In Christ, we have the hope that one day we will be with Him in heaven and free from this condition of sin. That is a glorious thought. And Christ confirms that He is our path to a relationship with the Father in John 14:6,

> "Jesus said to him, 'I am the way, and the truth, and the life; no one comes to the Father, but through me.'"

The way back to the tree of life, a spiritual life, is through Christ. In Christ, we have a spiritual life with the Father for eternity. In Romans 6:23 we read,

> "For the wages of sin is death, but the free gift of God is eternal life in Christ Jesus our Lord."

In keeping with my thought above, the wages of sin is spiritual death; a life apart from God. The eternal life in Christ is a spiritual life; a life with a relationship with God for eternity.

The penalty for sin is spiritual death. It isn't the penalty for some sin and not other sin, but the penalty for all sin is death.

In our justice system, the penalty for committing a crime is dependent on the severity of the crime. In God's justice system, there is only one penalty for any and all sin...spiritual death.

Apart from Christ we cannot enjoy a relationship with our Creator and God; He will not walk with us. It is not a separation from society with visitation rights. There are no visitation rights and it is complete separation from God. It is a very severe sentence and the sentence is for eternity!

Repeating Romans 3:23, "all have sinned and fall short of the glory of God." We all have sinned and deserve the death sentence. However, there is the finished work of Christ which saves those who believe.

Chapter 6

Finished Work of Christ

We often like to think that if we do enough good things, it will wipe away any of the bad things we have done. We are not seeking forgiveness for our sin. We are seeking a goodness that outweighs the badness. However, that does not address our sin.

There is a direct penalty for our sin. Death is required for God to extend forgiveness to the sinner. Blood must be shed.

God has demanded the death of an innocent one. God has demanded the sprinkling of blood of the one who dies as payment for the one who sins. Apart from the death payment, a man's sins cannot be forgiven.

In the Old Testament, the Israeli nation was constantly providing innocent animals for blood offerings for the sin of individuals and for the sin of the nation. The life of the animals was in the blood. So ultimately, what God was requiring was the sacrifice of the life of the innocent animal for the life of the guilty sinner. God was requiring an innocent life be sacrificed unto death for the forgiveness of sins.

I believe we can say the first sacrifice for man's sin occurred in Genesis 3:21 when we read,

> "And the Lord God made garments of skin for Adam and his wife, and clothed them."

Innocent blood was shed to cover man's nakedness (shame, sin).

The problem is that the sacrifice of animals never fully satisfied the penalty for sins and so needed to be constantly offered. The priest would sprinkle the sinner with the blood as a sign that the penalty for his sin had been borne by the innocent animal. However, the sprinkling of animal blood did not last. It was only a symbol for the real sacrifice that would be paid for our sins which was the death of the Son of God, Jesus Christ.

God planned for the ultimate sacrifice for the forgiveness of our sins. God planned to satisfy the penalty of spiritual death once and for all, so that we could have a relationship with the God of the Bible, our Creator and Father. God planned to walk with us again in the gardens of our lives.

Christ's sacrificial death was the plan and fulfills that penalty for our sin. He was without blemish. He was without flaw. He was without sin. He is the Son of God who takes away the sin of the world. John 1:29 reads,

> "The next day he saw Jesus coming to him, and said, "Behold, the Lamb of God who takes away the sin of the world!""

I believe there were two deaths experienced by Christ on the cross. There was the painful physical death of the crucifixion. And, there was the painful spiritual death or spiritual separation from God the Father when Christ proclaimed in Matthew 27:46,

> "My God, My God, why hast Thou forsaken Me?"

The physical death was the innocent blood for the forgiveness of our sins. Through Christ's physical death on the cross there was the shedding of innocent blood. When God looks at us, as believers, He sees the blood of Christ shed on our behalf and we are forgiven.

But remember, I believe the penalty of sin was spiritual death; and through that moment of spiritual death experienced by Christ on the cross, the penalty for sin was satisfied.

Both deaths were necessary; innocent blood needed to be shed and the penalty needed to be paid. Both were accomplished in the One, Jesus Christ.

Think on this: The Son of God, for a moment in time (the gospels of Mark and Luke tell us that this moment lasted for three hours) was separated from God the Father, in order that we might have eternal life; that we might spend eternity with God the Father. It was the ultimate sacrifice.

Christ's work did not end with dying on a cross. Christ rose from the dead. Christ demonstrated that there was life after death, and that life was ours in Him. Christ proved that he had power over death. Christ demonstrated that he had the power to give us life; spiritual life.

Christ ascended into heaven; He showed us where we would ultimately live for eternity. And after Christ ascended, the Spirit of God descended upon us as believers. As believers we are not alone to live out the Christian life, but we have the Spirit of God in us. Christ not only purchased our forgiveness of sin but, through the Holy Spirit, gives us the power to sin no more.

It is an overwhelming thought. I am still in awe that God did all that for me. He did all that for you. He did all that so He could walk with us.

Chapter 7

Closing Thoughts

God walking with us involves growing in our relationship with God the Father and learning to become overcomers in our struggle between our inane ability to sin and the power of the Holy Spirit of God within us as we seek to serve the Lord and to sin no more. But first, we need to be sure we are ready for the walk.

Do you believe God exists?

Do you believe you are a sinner?

Do you understand the penalty of your sin? Do you understand that you pay the penalty for your sin (eternal separation from God) or you accept the payment Christ completed on the cross?

Have you placed your faith in Christ? If you should die and come before God, and He asked you why He should let you into heaven, are you able to say because of what Christ did on the cross? If God was to ask me, my answer would be because of who I am in Christ. Christ paid the penalty for my sin. He purchased eternal life for me.

The title of this section is "Saving Faith." Someone who has placed his/her faith in Christ, a Christian, believes in the God of the Bible, repents of sin, accepts Christ's death for the forgiveness of sins, accepts Christ as Lord of one's life and submits to the Spirit of God to continue his/her life journey in Christ. And, it is a life journey with God walking with us.

If you have already placed your faith in Christ, I hope this book encourages you in your walk with Him. If you have not placed your faith in Christ, I offer this prayer for you to say so that you too can enjoy the fullness of God's love for you, the forgiveness of your sin, and know the power of the Spirit of God in your life; that you may begin your life journey in Christ with God walking with you.

Dear Lord, I acknowledge my sin. I acknowledge my inability to do anything about the penalty for my sin. I acknowledge by faith that Christ on the cross paid the penalty for my sin. By faith I place my life in Your hands. I ask that Christ be Lord of my life. I accept His death and resurrection on my behalf. I ask the Spirit of God to take residence in my life and cause me to grow in the likeness of Christ to the glory of God. I ask You to walk with me. Amen.

In closing, Isaiah 12:2:

> "Behold, God is my salvation, I will trust and not be afraid; For the Lord God is my strength and song, and He has become my salvation."

God's Unconditional Love

"For God so loved the world, that He gave His only begotten Son, that whoever believes in Him should not perish, but have eternal life (John 3:16)."

Chapter 8

Introduction

THE PATH GOD WALKS WITH US IS PAVED WITH GOD'S unconditional love. Everything we will ever be in Christ starts with His love toward us. His love will sustain us through the ups and downs of our Christian walks. Romans 8:37-39 says it so well,

> "But in all these things we overwhelmingly conquer through Him who loved us. For I am convinced that neither death, nor life, nor angels, nor principalities, nor things present, nor things to come, nor powers, nor height, nor depth, nor any other created thing, shall be able to separate us from the love of God, which is in Christ Jesus our Lord."

We will face difficulties in our individual walks with Christ, but nothing can separate us from God's love for us. It is a very comforting promise for us, as Christians. Others will fail us, but God will not! God walks with us.

We do not have to earn God's love but He freely gives it to us in Christ. Because He freely gives it, we cannot lose it. He loves us for eternity.

I watched a movie about the legendary track star, Jesse Owens. What struck me most about the man was his commitment to young men and women. If he saw a young person in distress, he would take them for a walk. He would get them out of the situation to talk and hopefully, gain a new perspective and then walk back. If you wanted to discuss something with Mr. Owens, you went for a walk.

Well, that is what God does with us. He takes us out of our perspective of a situation and gives us His perspective. He helps us see that the big problem in our little world, is a little problem in His big world.

Sometimes, literally, we go for a walk. And then He puts me back into the situation, hopefully now looking at it through His loving eyes and not my sinful eyes. And sometimes, we go for several walks; I can have some strong emotions. And the whole time He reminds me of the great love He has toward me.

Chapter 9

Is Always with Us

THE TRUTH IS THAT GOD IS ALWAYS WITH US; ALWAYS READY TO take that walk and shower us with His love; always ready to give us the strength through His Spirit to persevere. We do not walk the journey of our life in Christ alone. A verse that comforts me is Deuteronomy 31:6,

> "Be strong and courageous, do not be afraid or tremble at them, for the Lord your God is the one who goes with you. He will not fail you or forsake you."

I do not trust the world and do not trust most people in the world. I need God's reminder to be strong and courageous. I need the affirmation that He is with me and His love will never fail or forsake me.

If you are like me, you have had people who say they love you and fail you (let's be honest, we have also failed people). But God will not fail us. He will always love us and be with us, walking with us.

I was driving from San Bernardino, CA to Albuquerque, NM when my car had some engine problems. Because I was travelling, I ended up in a hotel in Arizona while a mechanic worked on the car. He thought he had fixed it, so the owner of the shop and I took it for a test drive...innocent enough, right?

Well, he suggested we visit a ghost town since for all practical purposes I was a tourist and I said sure. So, we turn off the driven path, and I do mean off the driven path (it was obvious cars did not pass this way often), and the car dies. I mean it just dies.

Well, I knew the routine, wait awhile and it will start again. I get out of the car to sit and wait. The owner decides to tell me how he could rape me and leave me for dead and no one would ever find my body. I nervously chuckled and said that he did not want to do that. He adamantly said that yes he thought about forcing himself on me.

So, I proceeded to let him know that God would know. He said that he didn't care. And I explained to him that I did care. God would be with me and would know where my body was placed. Someone, God, would know what he did. I also explained that he would have to live with the knowledge of what he did and answer to God one day.

Fortunately, he did nothing. (And note to self - think before you agree to go for a ride with someone you don't know.)

Now, I was scared and I was praying hard. But I also had a deep assurance that God was with me and He loved me. I found great comfort in knowing God loved me. God that day chose to protect me from harm. I wish I could help you grasp the strength I felt knowing God was with me and would not abandon me.

I still find great strength in knowing God loves me and is with me and will never leave me. There is absolutely nothing I can do to cause God to ever forsake me; to ever stop loving me. He has secured me as His child forever. John 10:27-30 says it so well what I felt that day and every day,

> "My sheep hear My voice, and I know them, and they follow Me; and I give eternal life to them, and they shall never perish; and no one shall snatch them out of My

> hand. My Father, who has given them to Me, is greater than all; and no one is able to snatch them out of the Father's hand. I and the Father are one."

He walks with me, hand in hand, like a loving Father. I picture God the Father reaching down and holding my hand while I walk this journey in Christ. And, nothing can cause Him to release the hold of love He has on me. His Spirit resides within me, so that I may more fully know Him and His love. It is amazing. I believe the same for you!

As we walk in Christ together, I hope to help you gain new perspective of God's unconditional love and acceptance of you and encourage you in His walk with you. Bottom line, I want His walk with you to be filled with His unconditional love for you.

Chapter 10

Experienced

UNDERSTANDING GOD'S UNCONDITIONAL LOVE OF ME WAS A process. I did not feel 'lovable,' especially not by an almighty God. But God does love me unconditionally and walks with me while I continually learn to believe it. I still need the occasionally reminder and, fortunately, God does not get tired of telling me how much He unconditionally loves me.

Now understand, I knew God loved me; it was the unconditional part that was difficult. I thought I had to continually earn God's love and work for any blessings God should bestow upon me. I didn't understand that God might do something for me simply out of His love for me.

I did not understand that His unconditional love is a promise in God's relationship with His children. He and I had several walks as I learned the truth of His love toward me and toward you. 1 John 4:18, 19 reads,

> "There is no fear in love; but perfect love casts out fear, because fear involves punishment, and the one who

> fears is not perfected in love. We love, because He first loved us."

Fear was an accurate description of my relationship with the Lord. I knew what my earthly father was capable of, how much more my heavenly Father. But God the Father was different. He loved me unconditionally and needed nothing in return from me for that love.

Fear was me not trusting His love for me. So God and I went for a walk and I thought of the passage in Luke, specifically Luke 16:10 which reads,

> "He who is faithful in a very little thing is faithful also in much..."

The thought I had was that if this was true of people it was also true of God. If I saw God faithful in little things because He loved me, then I could believe Him faithful in big things because He loved me. We needed to build a relationship of trust.

I want to be clear about something, I wasn't trying to get God to do things for me, I was trying to build my faith in a loving God. I did not create a want list, but rather tried to pick simple 'needs' requests to build my faith that God really did care about the details of my life and really did love me because He chose to love me.

I still remember the first thing for which I asked. I was a missionary at the time and raising financial support was definitely a weakness in my faith. So, I asked God for something financial to show me he cared about my finances. I was not specific, I just asked for something. Well, God has a great sense of humor because I got a bill in the mail. It was financial.

Over the next several weeks, each day I would ask God for something and He would faithfully answer. Some requests were more specific than others. One request was for help as I tried to transport a projector and screen across the college campus where I was ministering. Well, a student saw me (a student I did not know) and he offered to help. I smiled and said thank you, Lord.

It was overwhelming to see God work on my behalf in the insignificant details of my life because He loved me. Were they insignificant details? Not really, but when I thought of the almighty God having to run the world and care for so many, me needing help getting a projector and screen across campus seemed a bit insignificant. But it wasn't insignificant to God, because He loved me. I felt significant. And, I still feel significant.

It is an amazing thought to me that God does things for me and answers my prayers simply because He loves me. He doesn't care for me because He wants something in return. He does it simply because He loves me in Christ. It is in Christ that He loves me. Even as I write this I am overcome with emotion. God loves me. God loves you. It is amazing.

As the concept developed, I realized God knew better than me what I needed any given day and so rather than provide an avenue for God to show me His love, I just asked for hugs. On a human level we sometimes just need someone to give us a hug. I have people in my life from whom I sometimes request a hug. We need hugs. So, I tell God I need a hug from Him. And you know what, I get my hugs! I love my hugs!!

One night I had this dream, a dream probably every single woman has had, that I was about to get married. We are at the altar getting ready to take our vows and I ask him if he is sure that he wants to get married. He says no and that he wasn't sure he was doing the right thing. We called off the wedding. Well, I woke up feeling so very rejected. The emotion of the dream was real. So, I asked God for a special hug.

I am laughing as I write His answer. I went home for lunch and was in just the giddiest mood. I told God that if I didn't know any better I would think I had fallen in love. And then I remembered my request for a special hug. God romanced me. He made me feel like a loved woman of value. What a loving God. He cares about the things we care about.

Chapter 11

Expressed

WHENEVER GOD IS TEACHING ME SOMETHING ABOUT HIS relationship with me, He is also teaching me about my relationship to others. This is the wonderful thing about God walking with us, He trusts us with His work. God entrusts us with His most important work, saving and healing lives. Referring back to 1 John 4:19,

> "We love, because He first loved us."

God wants us to love. First He loves us and from the strength of His unconditional love, we are to love others. The passage in John 15:12-17 expresses it so well:

> "This is My commandment, that you love one another, just as I have loved you. Greater love has no one than this, that one lay down his life for his friends. You are My friends, if you do what I command you. No longer do I call you slaves, for the slave does not know what his master is doing; but I have called you friends, for all things that I have heard from My Father I have made

> known to you. You did not choose Me, but I chose you, and appointed you, that you should go and bear fruit, and that your fruit should remain, that whatever you ask of the Father in My name, He may give. This I command you, that you love one another."

Here is how it works. When we love someone, we want to do something to show our love. Well, we get so filled with God's love, we want to do something to show God our love for Him. God says we can show our love for Him by loving one another. I believe He wants us to love others unconditionally just as He loves us.

He did not command us to work. He commanded us to love one another as He loved us. I find when my heart is lacking love that I need to go back to my relationship with God and let Him love me. When I am tuned into God's love for me, loving others is easier.

I believe when we understand more fully God's love for us, we need less from others and are able to love more freely. When 'me' is more interested in me than others, it is time for God and I to take a walk and discuss His love for me. His love fills me so I can love.

In Christ, God loves you unconditionally. Allow that to fill you and complete you. Your ability to love will overflow from your love relationship with God the Father. Experience His love for you so you can express His love to others.

Chapter 12

Closing Thoughts

I HAVE CHALLENGED PEOPLE TO ASK GOD FOR A HUG. IT IS AMAZING to me how few people do. They are uncomfortable with the thought and yet they will ask each other for hugs. I think God's love scares us. I think it scares us for different reasons.

My fear was that he was going to set me up for disappointment. I would come to believe in His love and then fear He would desert me when I needed Him most. God has never failed me nor forsaken me. Others, I believe, fear what God might ask them to do.

People have abused our love and a hug is a very scary thing. Maybe, you need a different symbol of God's love. Maybe it's time to take a walk with God and explore this area of His walk with you.

God's love is safe. Christ died on the cross to demonstrate His love. Like I did, ask God to demonstrate His pure unconditional love toward you. Let Him show you His love. It required small steps of faith to get me to the place of security in His love that I am today. But there are still days when I need my hugs. What is a small step you can take?

God is patient. He wants you to know how much He loves you in Christ. Maybe all you can do right now is to simply ask Him to help you take that first step of faith. He will walk with you. He will walk as slow or as fast as you are able. And He will pause as you need to pause.

Once you start to feel the love of God poured out in your heart, you will never want to turn back. It will be the sweetest thing in your life. Remember what Romans 5:8 tells us:

> "But God demonstrates His own love toward us, in that while we were yet sinners, Christ died for us."

God's Unconditional Acceptance

"just as He chose us in Him before the foundation of the world, that we should be holy and blameless before Him (Ephesians 1:4)"

Chapter 13

Introduction

As I was writing this chapter I felt the weight of the message. Understanding God's acceptance of me, in Christ, apart from my works has been a difficult concept for me. But, God does unconditionally accept me in Christ. God does unconditionally accept you in Christ.

Right now, as I write this, in God's walk with me I am having to place my trust in God's acceptance of me. Others have made me feel unacceptable and I need God's assurance that I am enough. Wonderful thing is that God walks me through the pain and doesn't just say that I should already know that He accepts me in Christ. He knows I hurt and so He walks with me as I heal.

God's walk with us can be quite baffling. It is the sweetest, most wonderful thing in our lives; and it can also be just plain difficult. But I am getting ahead of myself.

I had a Christian boss who once asked me what I had given to God for which to build my trust of Him. I was dumbfounded. The last thing God needed was suggestions from me. He had a full list of items for which I needed to trust Him. That is how I feel about works and God's acceptance; He does not need help from me.

God has fully accepted me in Christ so there is nothing further I need to do. The measuring tool He uses for my acceptability and for your acceptability is Christ's finished work. Our unconditional acceptance by God was fully purchased by Christ's sacrifice on the cross.

I don't need to come up with a list of works for God; God has planned my good works in Christ. And those good works have nothing to do with me earning favor from God but have everything to do with God's good pleasure. The Apostle Paul tells us in Philippians 2:13:

> "for it is God who is at work in you, both to will and to work for His good pleasure."

At this point, I do believe I need to be clear about the consequences of sin in our lives. Sin does create a problem in our relationship with God. It does create a brokenness in that relationship.

Sin does not make us unacceptable to God because of Christ's finished work on the cross. Christ paid the penalty for sin, so God could unconditionally accept us as His children. God does not stop accepting us when we sin, but we do stop experiencing that acceptance.

We need to confess our sins, not because God needs us to (He already knows), but because we need to. The only thing that can erase our sense of guilt is forgiveness. Confession allows us to experience forgiveness and God's unconditional acceptance.

There was a point in my life that guilt was wearing me down. The intriguing thing is that I wasn't guilty but I felt the guilt for the sin that was committed against me. I went to God the Father and asked Him to replace my guilt with His forgiveness. The issue wasn't whether I was guilty or not, but that I needed to feel forgiven to be free from the guilt. God answered my prayer.

Now, there have been numerous times when I have also been very guilty and needed His forgiveness. 1 John 1:9 says it so well,

> "If we confess our sins, He is faithful and righteous to forgive us our sins and to cleanse us from all unrighteousness."

God wants to replace our guilt with forgiveness. God wants us to fully experience a relationship of unconditional acceptance by Him. He does not want us to worry about earning or losing His acceptance. He wants us to enjoy it! He wants us to enjoy Him walking with us.

Chapter 14

Not As A Result of Works

Our unconditional acceptance is not the result of our works but the finished work of Christ. Let's read a few verses together:

Ephesians 2:8, 9:

> "For by grace you have been saved through faith; and that not of yourselves, it is the gift of God; not as result of works, so that no one may boast. For we are His workmanship, created in Christ Jesus for good works, which God prepared beforehand, that we should walk in them."

Romans 3:24:

> "being justified as a gift by His grace through the redemption which is in Christ Jesus;"

Romans 11:5, 6:

> "In the same way then, there has also come to be at the present time a remnant according to God's gracious choice. But if it is by grace, it is no longer on the basis of works, otherwise grace is no longer grace."

I chose these verses to focus on the fact that our works are not required for us to have a relationship with God. Our relationship with God is solely based on the finished work of Christ. Christ's work is why we have a relationship with God for eternity.

We cannot add to Christ's work or subtract from it. We can, however, not fully enjoy it. And that, my dear friends, is one of the reasons God take walks with us, so we keep our focus on Him and the finished work of Christ.

I don't think anything strikes a nerve in me faster than when one someone discusses my "works" as a Christian. My "works" are not my responsibility. Note what verse Ephesians 2:10 says,

> "For we are His workmanship, created in Christ Jesus for good works, which God prepared beforehand, that we should walk in them."

I am God's workmanship in Christ. God prepared beforehand the good works that I should walk in them. The good works are not my doing. I am not my own workmanship. God is the author of my faith and my Christian walk with Him.

Remember that time when I was learning to trust God to do simple things in my life just to show me He loved me. Well, He was also teaching me that my faithfulness was more important than the actual results of my faithfulness.

I needed the projector and screen to show a movie that would introduce students to a faith in Christ. It was my turn to show the movie.

Well, it's time for the movie to start and there was not a single student. I wasn't sure what to do. I prayed and started the movie. By the end of the movie, more students attended this showing than any other showing. By faith, I started the movie; I was faithful. God did the rest.

The concept of works is a challenge for believers today and for the church. We measure each other by results. God does not measure by results. 1 Samuel 16:7 is a verse I quote to myself often as I feel judged by others:

> "But the Lord said to Samuel, "Do not look at his appearance or at the height of his stature, because I have rejected him; for God sees not as man sees, for man looks at the outward appearance, but the Lord looks at the heart.""

Often, we judge God's acceptance of ourselves and other Christians by our resume of good works. God doesn't. God accepts us based on Christ's resume. God would rather have the greatest heart for Him less the 'great' works than the greatest works less the heart.

God wants our hearts. Good works result from our heart relationship with God. And, our heart relationship is based on the complete unconditional acceptance of us by God through the finished work of Christ.

God does promise we will have good works (Ephesians 2:9) and that we will bear fruit:

John 15:5:

> "I am the vine, you are the branches; he who abides in Me, and I in him, he bears much fruit; for apart from Me you can do nothing."

Galatians 5:22, 23:

> "But the fruit of the Spirit is love, joy, peace, patience, kindness, goodness, faithfulness, gentleness, self-control; against such things there is no law."

If you notice, the good works and the fruit that we will bear is directly related to our God; either the Son of God or the Spirit of God. And notice in Galatians that the list is about the quality of our personality and not the quality of our works; works aren't mentioned.

God is more concerned with who we are in Christ then what we do. Transforming our hearts in Christ is the real work that God seeks to accomplish in us. Our "works" are a natural benefit of God's work in us. It's amazing how people respond when they know they are truly acceptable and don't need to change to be acceptable.

During my first experience as a manager, another department came to me because they wanted an employee of mine. It was basically a promotion for my employee so I was more than happy to agree. In return they were giving me one of their employees. I had a lot of respect for that employee so I was quite pleased.

Well, before I said yes, they felt it was important that I knew some of the employee's shortcomings. To be honest, I could not believe what they thought were shortcomings which had nothing to do with his ability to do the job or get along with people. He was somehow less than acceptable and they were hoping I would have more success in changing him. Well, you have probably read enough to know my thoughts on 'changing' someone.

This employee was older than me and had a strong walk with God from what I could see. If God did not feel a need to change him, I sure didn't. I thoroughly enjoyed working with this gentleman. He was great.

Well, the other department perceived a change in him and wanted to know what I did. I told them I accepted him. They said okay but what did you do. I said I made it safe for him to be himself; I accepted him. He didn't change; he just felt safe to be himself. It was a valuable lesson for me. Unconditional acceptance is powerful.

Chapter 15

God Chose Us

WE ARE TRAINED FROM AN EARLY AGE THAT OUR PERFORMANCE is important if we expect to be chosen. Chosen for the football team, chosen for the job or promotion, chosen for the political position, etc. Often character isn't important, just our performance.

Well, it is different with God. Read Ephesians 2:8, 9 again. God saved us purely from His heart and it had nothing to do with our performance. The verses say it was a free gift. It was free for us but it cost God dearly. Christ endured death on a cross for that free gift. That free gift is in Christ's finished work.

When you consider what Christ endured so that you could have a relationship with God the Father, do you really think you can do anything greater to gain that relationship? Do you really think your works can measure up to that standard?

I am so glad my works do not have to measure up to the standard of Christ. I am so glad that my works are God's responsibility. If I had to do works to God's measure of standard, I would certainly fail. But, I don't have to. God has unconditionally accepted me and does His work through me in Christ.

John 15:16 tells us:

> "You did not choose Me, but I chose you, and appointed you, that you should go and bear fruit, and that your fruit should remain, that whatever you ask of the Father in My name, He may give to you."

God chose me before I did anything. He appointed me to bear fruit; to have good works. This was all planned by God. It is not something I accomplish; it is something God accomplishes through me.

One of my favorite verses is Matthew 20:28 which reads,

> "just as the Son of Man did not come to be served, but to serve, and to give His life a ransom for many."

I just love this verse and quote it often. When people try to tell me what I should be doing for the Lord, I quote this verse. Christ did not come to be served by me; He came to serve me. He did not come to get me to do good works. He came to do His finished work on the cross. He came to save me from sin and give me eternal life. He came to save you and give you eternal life.

I have learned that when I let Christ serve me; when I let God's unconditional love and acceptance fill me; I see God do amazing things through me. And I am glad to let God have the glory because what He accomplishes through me is greater than anything I could have imagined doing. I am at my best when it is not me and it is the Spirit of God through me.

Furthering the concept of Christ serving us, please read John 13: 5-8:

> "Then He poured water into the basin, and began to wash the disciples' feet, and to wipe them with the towel with which He was girded. And so He came to Simon Peter. He said to Him, "Lord, do You wash my

> feet?" Jesus answered and said to him, "What I do you do not realize now, but you shall understand hereafter." Peter said to Him, "Never shall You wash my feet!" Jesus answered him, "If I do not wash you, you have no part with Me.""

Jesus, Lord and God, washed the feet of His disciples. He did the job of a servant. Later, in John 13:12-15 Jesus goes on to say,

> "Do you know what I have done to you? You call Me Teacher and Lord; and you are right, for so I am. If I then, the Lord and the Teacher, washed your feet, you also ought to wash one another's feet. For I gave you an example that you also should do as I did to you."

You want to know what works the Lord wants. He want works from our love relationship with Him in service to others. He wants works that emanate from such an assurance of God's acceptance of us in Christ we can freely serve others.

Chapter 16

Closing Thoughts

As I write this I am aware of how much more I still need to grow in God's unconditional acceptance of me. I have been well trained to perform.

When I struggle with the demands to do more (that I have not done enough), I need God's walks with me to reaffirm his unconditional acceptance of me. If in Christ, I have done my best, then I have done enough regardless of what others might want from me.

I had to deal with a boss who felt the need to keep his employees on edge about their performance at work. The constant critiquing and having work being judged caused me much pain. In service to the Lord, you never want to be perceived as not doing your best. I had done the best job I could do. My performance just was not good enough for my boss.

As I prayed and God walked with me, I knew that I had done all I could do. I could not have done a better job than the job I had done and the job that I had done was good. I was good at my job. I knew God accepted me and my performance.

I thought of Joseph's experience while a slave in the house of Potiphar (Genesis 39) and realized that doing the right thing does not always lead to approval by man. Sometimes people have other motives. I did not do my job for the approval of man; I did it as unto the Lord, in obedience to the Lord.

After much prayer, I resigned my position. If my best was not good enough and if I gave all I could and it still was not enough then the right thing for me to do was to resign. In Christ, I answered to God for my performance in my job.

Fortunately, God had other plans for me; He had other works for me. Through it all, I knew God unconditionally accepted me and approved of me. It comforted me significantly that I was accepted and approved by my God.

Do you find yourself trying to earn God's pleasure? Do you find yourself trying to be like the 'better' Christian so you can be acceptable to God? God only wants you. He wants you to be all you can be in Christ.

Do you have people in your life who accept you and provide a safe place to be you? Are you a safe place for your friends? Do you accept them?

I have great people in my life who accept me, encourage me and are honest with me. They walk with me when I need the support. Hopefully, I do the same for them.

God has unconditionally accepted us in Christ. Can we do any less but to accept one another?

> "Wherefore, accept one another, just as Christ also accepted us to the glory of God (Romans 15:7)."

Reality of Sin

"If we say that we have not sinned, we make Him a liar, and His word is not in us (1 John 1:10)."

Chapter 17

Introduction

God's walks with us will require honesty. A difficult topic for Christians is the presence of sin in our lives. Sin is a reality. Fortunately, forgiveness is also a reality for the Christian.

As we look at the reality of sin, please remember forgiveness is God's plan for us. To understand God's healing power of forgiveness for our hearts we need to discuss obvious sins, sins of the heart and the power of sin. We need to understand sin to be set free from it.

Somehow we think that if we sin it makes us less of a Christian. And yet, sin we will. And, God will continually forgive us in Christ. I am not saying we have permission to sin, I am just saying we are sinners.

Sometimes I think we are confused about sin. We create this image of the perfect Christian and we believe it is sin if we do not measure up to this perfect Christian. I want to clear something up right now, there is not a perfect Christian. There is a perfect Christ, but not a perfect Christian. Being imperfect is not a sin.

We should not be surprised when we sin or others sin. The particular sin might surprise us, but the fact that we sin should not be a surprise. It is not a surprise to God. Every day I place myself before the throne of God's mercy and grace and ask Him to live His life in and through me. And, He does; He walks with me.

I am tempted and struggle with sin every day. Some sins I have been able to avoid, but being human I have my sinful moments and God and I go for a walk. As promised, God always forgives me.

I say in Christ I have avoided some sins because I believe we are all capable of all sin known to man. Why don't more people commit what we consider the bigger sins; the ones that get people put in jail? I think it is due to the restraint of God's grace. God's grace restrains non-believers as well as believers. I rely on God's grace in Christ to restrain me.

A passage I often ponder when considering my own sin and the sin of others is John 8:3-11:

> "And the scribes and the Pharisees brought a woman caught in adultery, and having set her in the midst, they said to Him, "Teacher, this woman has been caught in adultery, in the very act. Now in the Law Moses commanded us to stone such women; what then do You say?" And they were saying this, testing Him, in order that they might have grounds for accusing Him. But Jesus stooped down, and with His finger wrote on the ground. But when they persisted in asking Him, He straightened up, and said to them, "He who is without sin among you, let him be the first to throw a stone at her." And again He stooped down, and wrote on the ground. And when they heard it, they began to go out one by one, beginning with the older ones, and He was left alone, and the woman, where she had been, in the midst. And straightening up, Jesus said to her, "Woman, where are they? Did no one condemn you?" And she said, "No one, Lord." And Jesus said, "Neither

do I condemn you; go your way. From now on sin no more.""

As we discuss the topic of sin I want to us to keep in mind some ideas from this passage -

- We should not be quick to condemn. We are guilty of sin.
- God did not condemn.
- Jesus asked her to sin no more. I often have wondered about that order to "sin no more" but I think the woman knew that Jesus was instructing her to not commit the sin of adultery again. He won't condemn us but He does expect us to stop committing the same sins.

Chapter 18

Obvious Sins

SIN CANNOT BE DISCUSSED WITHOUT PRESENTING THE TEN Commandments. The Ten Commandments are very much a part of the Christian faith. Growing up Catholic, I went through the list when I had to go to confession. I knew I had to confess breaking one of them. One time I could not think of anything to confess, so I lied, so I could confess the lie.

Let's read Exodus 20:1-26 (I will space between the Ten Commandments as we go through the text):

> "Then God spoke all these words, saying, "I am the Lord your God, who brought you out of the land of Egypt, out of the house of slavery.
>
> You shall have no other gods before me.
>
> You shall not make for yourself an idol, or any likeness of what is in heaven above or on the earth beneath or in the water under the earth. You shall not worship them or serve them; for I, the Lord your God, am a jealous

God, visiting the iniquity of the fathers on the children, on the third and the fourth generations of those who hate Me, but showing lovingkindness to thousands, to those who love Me and keep My commandments.

You shall not take the name of the Lord your God in vain, for the Lord will not leave him unpunished who takes His name in vain.

Remember the Sabbath day, to keep it holy. Six days you shall labor and do all your work, but the seventh day is a Sabbath of the Lord your God; in it you shall not do any work, you or your son or your daughter, your male or your female servant or your cattle or your sojourner who stays with you. For in six days the Lord made the heavens and the earth, the sea and all that is in them, and rested on the seventh day; therefore the Lord blessed the Sabbath day and made it holy.

Honor your father and your mother, that your days may be prolonged in the land which the Lord your God gives you.

You shall not murder.

You shall not commit adultery.

You shall not steal.

You shall not bear false witness against your neighbor.

You shall not covet your neighbor's house; you shall not covet your neighbor's wife or his male servant or his female servant or his ox or his donkey or anything that belongs to your neighbor.""

It is a thorough list when you reflect on the commandments. The first few address our relationship to God and the rest address our relationship with others.

The commandment to keep the Sabbath day holy is a unique commandment to me. I have two thoughts on this commandment. First of all, we need a day of rest from our labors. If God could rest from His labor, we can trust God and rest from our labor. Secondly, by not resting, are we then not trusting God to make provision for our lives?

Before you think you are doing pretty good as it relates to keeping the Ten Commandments, I want to share James 2:10,

> "For whoever keeps the whole law and yet stumbles in one point, he has become guilty of all."

That is a powerful statement that 'he has become guilty of all." We often think it is a little sin so we don't have to worry too much. But this verse in James tells us that one sin makes us "guilty of all." So, should we go ahead and commit the worst of them? NO! I encourage you to read Romans 6 which addresses this question so well.

When I ponder that we are guilty of all, it humbles me. It reminds me that apart from the grace of God, I could break any of the commandments listed. It also reminds me of how much I need Christ in my life. It reminds me of how much I need God walking with me.

I think we often are not aware of the sins we commit. However, we are committing sins. We are imperfect people.

Sins have an impact on our relationship with God and ourselves and others. We need to address our sins and be ever on the alert; because, we are always one second away from committing another sin. We need to pray as the Psalmist in Psalms 139:23, 24:

> "Search me, O God, and know my heart; Try me and know my anxious thoughts; and see if there be any hurtful way in me, and lead me in the everlasting way."

We need to ever be mindful of the choices we make and how they can lead to sin. Our actions do have consequences.

Please understand, I believe only God's grace through His Spirit can keep us from sin. However, I also believe we need to be on the alert and rely on God's power to resist. Sin is serious.

Chapter 19

Sins of the Heart

Our conversation is about to get a little more personal. Sins of the heart are more personal because they often are the ones we can hide from others. Remember 1 Samuel 16:7:

> "But the Lord said to Samuel, "Do not look at his appearance or at the height of his stature, because I have rejected him; for God sees not as man sees, for man looks at the outward appearance, but the Lord looks at the heart.""

This verse not only applies to the goodness in an individual's heart but also the sin. And while others may not see what is in our hearts; God does. God knows the sin that lurks within our hearts.

It is a scary thing to think someone can look into our hearts and thoughts and know everything about us. Well, God can and does. I can hide from you, but I cannot hide from God. Adam and Eve tried to hide from God, but He knew.

There are times in my Christian life that when friends ask me how I'm doing and I say God is letting me see my humanness. What I am really saying is that God is letting me see that I am not perfect and have some real issues which He needs to address in my life.

God is committed to me and knows within my heart there is sin interfering with the full joy I can have in my relationship with Him and others. He wants to create a pure heart within me. He wants to create a pure heart within you.

Jesus in Matthew 5:27, 28 says this,

> "You have heard that it was said, 'You shall not commit adultery'; but I say to you, that everyone who looks on a woman to lust for her has committed adultery with her already in his heart."

This truth applies to every one of the Ten Commandments. Sin is first committed in our hearts before it's ever outwardly committed. What this verse is telling us is that we don't actually have to do it for it to be sin, we can commit the sin in our hearts; makes me want to guard my heart. This is why I need God to create a pure heart within me.

So, since we have already committed the sin in our hearts should we go ahead and follow through? NO! The goal is to stop and confess the sin before it becomes worse and causes more damage. The goal is to flee temptation as it says in Hebrews 12:1:

> "let us also lay aside every encumbrance, and the sin which so easily entangles us"

When I think of fleeing sin, I think of Joseph in Genesis 39:7-13,

> "And it came about after these events that his master's wife looked with desire at Joseph, and she said, 'Lie with me.' But he refused and said to his master's wife, 'Behold, with me here, my master does not concern himself with anything in the house, and he has put all

> that he owns in my charge. There is no one greater in this house than I, and he has withheld nothing from me except you, because you are his wife. How then could I do this great evil, and sin against God?' And it came about as she spoke to Joseph day after day, that he did not listen to her to lie beside her, or be with her. Now it happened one day that he went into the house to do his work, and none of the men of the household was there inside. And she caught him by his garment, saying, 'Lie with me!' And he left his garment in her hand and fled, and went outside."

Joseph wasn't tempted once or twice, but day after day. There are two things I notice about Joseph's response to the temptation; first, he would not sin against God and secondly, he fled. And think about it, she had such a hold on Joseph that he left his garment in her hand when he fled; it wasn't just innocent flirting.

By the way, the Ten Commandments had not yet been written on the tablets of stone. But, they had been written on the heart of Joseph because he had a relationship with his God.

The best example of this concept of the condition of the heart before God is Matthew 23:27, 28:

> "Woe to you, scribes and Pharisees, hypocrites! For you are like whitewashed tombs which on the outside appear beautiful, but inside they are full of dead men's bones and all uncleanness. Even so you too outwardly appear righteous to men, but inwardly you are full of hypocrisy and lawlessness."

Outwardly, the Pharisees kept the Ten Commandments. Inwardly, they were very far from God. Outwardly, they were righteous. Inwardly, they were full of sin. We need to be careful to not just look at the outward expression of sin and have God examine our hearts. I want to be a Joseph; not a Pharisee.

We need to pray to God for the protection of our hearts. We need to ask Him to write his commandments on our hearts.

Chapter 20

Personal Sins

Now, there are sins that are sins regardless of the individual such as the Ten Commandments. And, there are sins for some individuals that are not sins for others. Those sins have to do with the individual's relationship with the Lord and/or the church he/she attends. Differences are okay until we force them on other believers.

I use to donate blood on a regular basis. Another believer told me it was a sin to donate blood. My response was that Christ shed His blood to give me life; He set the example for me to give my blood to save a life.

It was okay with me that he saw it as sin for him, but it did not make it sin for me. We need to be careful when we make something that is sin for us, sin for another. The Apostle Paul addresses this concept in 1 Corinthians 8:4-8:

> "Therefore concerning the eating of things sacrificed to idols, we know that there is no such thing as an idol in the world, and that there is no God but one. For even if there are so-called gods whether in heaven or on earth,

> as indeed there are many gods and many lords, yet for us, there is but one God, the Father, from whom are all things, and we exist for Him; and one Lord, Jesus Christ, by whom are all things, and we exist through Him. However, not all men have this knowledge; but some being accustomed to the idol until now, eat food as if it were sacrificed to an idol; and their conscience being weak is defiled. But food will not commend us to God; we are neither the worse if we do not eat, nor the better if we do eat."

Paul goes on to say we should not cause our brother to stumble.

I believe the point Paul is trying to make is that for some it was sin to eat the meat sacrificed to idols and for some it was not. Paul accepted that and, I believe, left it up to each believer to decide for himself. I like how he basically says that neither is right and neither is wrong. The important principle was to have a clear conscience before God; a pure heart.

We need to be careful not to put rules God has for our walks with Him on others. We need to be careful to not take theirs upon us. This is where we really have to be careful in our judgment. I am always mindful of the woman they were so eager to stone. Christ basically said only he without sin could cast a stone. I am not without sin.

Chapter 21

Power of Sin

WE TYPICALLY ONLY TALK ABOUT THE ACT OF SINNING AND NOT the power of sin in our lives. Our sinful nature is alive and well and seeking it's pleasure. It is only as we rely on the Spirit of Christ (the Holy Spirit) in us do we keep our sinful natures in submission to the will of God. It is only through the power of the Holy Spirit that we do not succumb to the power of sin in our lives.

The Apostle Paul addresses this whole concept of the power of sin in our lives in Romans 7. As we read these verses bear in mind that Paul has been walking in the Lord and ministering for the Lord for years. He has already written several of his epistles and has endured much hardship for the Lord. The passage I am referring to is Romans 7:9-25:

> "And I was once alive apart from the law; but when the commandment came, sin became alive, and I died; and this commandment, which was to result in life, proved to result in death for me; for sin, taking opportunity through the commandment, deceived me, and through it killed me. So then, the Law is holy, and the commandment is holy and righteous and good.

> Therefore did that that which is good become a cause of death for me? May it never be! Rather it was sin, in order that it might be shown to be sin by effecting my death through that which is good, that through the commandment sin might become utterly sinful. For we know that the Law is spiritual; but I am of flesh, sold into bondage to sin. For that which I am doing, I do not understand; for I am not practicing what I would like to do, but I am doing the very thing I hate. But if I do the very thing I do not wish to do, I agree with the Law, confessing that it is good. So now, no longer am I the one doing it, but sin which indwells me. For I know that nothing good dwells in me, that is, in my flesh; for the wishing is present in me, but the doing of the good is not. For the good that I wish, I do not do; but I practice the very evil that I do not wish. But if I am doing the very thing I do not wish, I am no longer the one doing it, but sin which dwells in me. I find then the principle that evil is present in me, the one who wishes to do good. For I joyfully concur with the law of God in the inner man, but I see a different law in the members of my body, waging war against the law of my mind, and making me a prisoner of the law of sin which is in my members. Wretched man that I am! Who will set me free from the body of this death? Thanks be to God through Jesus Christ our Lord! So then, on the one hand I myself with my mind am serving the law of God, but on the other, with my flesh the law of sin."

This is a very powerful passage; and if it is true of Paul, it is definitely true of us. Fortunately, Paul provides us with the victory to this battle - Jesus Christ our Lord. Paul recognized the power of sin in his life; do we?

I know I struggle with the power of sin in my life. I have some strong emotions and sometimes it is a battle to get them to submit to the will of God. God and I do a lot of walking and talking. I think this is when I have my most intimate prayer is when my emotions battle the hardest. It should not cause us to question our faith when we struggle but drive us to the power of God.

The Apostle Paul says in Philippians 3:12-14:

> "Not that I have already obtained it, or have already become perfect, but I press on in order that I may lay hold of that for which also I was laid hold of by Christ Jesus. Brethren, I do not regard myself as having laid hold of it yet; but one thing I do, forgetting what lies behind and reaching forward to what lies ahead, I press on toward the goal for the prize of the upward call of God in Christ Jesus."

We need to recognize the power of sin in our lives. We need to recognize the power of the Holy Spirit in our lives. And as Paul says, we need to press on. God has given us the Holy Spirit so we can press on.

The battle is real. We sometimes simplify sin as just a choice, but Paul clearly talks about the battle between the law of sin and law of God in the believer. But, the victory is ours through Jesus Christ through the power of the Holy Spirit which follows in Romans 8. Later on, we will be discussing Romans 8. God has provided a solution.

Chapter 22

Closing Thoughts

THE DISCOURAGING NEWS IS THAT WE ARE STILL SINNERS. THE encouraging news is that we have victory over sin and the power of sin in Christ Jesus. We are always a second away from sin but, the power of the Spirit of God is not a second away from us. He is with us now giving us victory in each second as He walks with us.

Sin is not a topic we like discussing. But it is an important truth. Ignoring the truth about sin will not make it go away. It will actually make it stronger. We get victory over sin by confessing and allowing ourselves to feel God's forgiveness.

Do you understand the power of sin in your life and the need for the power of the Holy Spirit? Do you even realize that you are still a sinner? There are those who believe we no longer sin once Christ becomes our Lord. I defer to Paul.

I close with Hebrews 12:1, 2:

> "Therefore, since we have so great a cloud of witnesses surrounding us, let us also lay aside every encumbrance, and the sin which so easily entangles us, and let us run with endurance the race that is set before us, fixing our

eyes on Jesus, the author and perfecter of faith, who for the joy set before Him endured the cross, despising the shame, and has sat down at the right hand of the throne of God."

Forgiveness Heals

"As far as the east is from the west, so far has He removed our transgressions from us (Psalms 103:12)."

Chapter 23

Introduction

AFTER TALKING ABOUT SIN, IT IS IMPERATIVE THAT WE TALK about the healing power of confession and forgiveness. God does not want us to stay downcast because of our sin; He wants us to know the forgiveness we have in Christ.

Since I am in Christ, I am not responsible to solve the problem of sin in my life. If you are in Christ, you are not responsible to solve the problem of sin in your life. If you are not in Christ (see truth - Saving Faith), then you have a problem with the sin in your life.

God has provided the solution to our sin through the finished work of Christ. Step by step, moment by moment, God the Father douses us with the healing power of His forgiveness. I am forgiven in Christ. You are forgiven in Christ.

Sin and forgiveness is something we must confess daily. The guilt from our sin is a cancer to our hearts. It is why people become bitter or stay angry or avoid intimacy or...

As Christians we can be robbed of the joy of our relationship with God the Father and others because of the guilt we have from our sin.

Forgiveness heals the cancer of our hearts. Forgiveness allows us to experience God walking with us.

I believe forgiveness is how God perfects us in Christ. He roots out that which is sinful in us and fills us with Christ. Forgiveness is God's grace toward us in perfect love.

Forgiveness is like a good buffing process for a wax job on a car. I thought of buffing because a friend was buffing his car and was excited because he could see his reflection in the car.

I think forgiveness is the buffing process by which Christ sees His reflection in us. Forgiveness just may be the best way that we allow a world to see Christ in us.

My favorite verse for the confession and forgiveness of sin is 1 John 1:8, 9:

> "If we say that we have no sin, we are deceiving ourselves, and the truth is not in us. If we confess our sins, He is faithful and righteous to forgive us our sins and to cleanse us from all unrighteousness."

He forgives us and he cleanses us (he buffs us). Sin often does leave us feeling dirty; like there is something wrong with us. We need forgiveness. We need cleansing. We need healing.

For most of my Christian life, whenever I thought about healing, I only thought about the need for physical healing; healing of diseases, sicknesses and infirmities. However, now in God's walk with me, I have come to discover a more important healing. I believe in the healing power of forgiveness. We need forgiveness from God and from one another to heal.

As God walks with us, sin, confession and forgiveness will be daily companions. Sin is still present in our lives and in our worlds, therefore, confession of sin and forgiveness needs to be present in our lives and in our worlds. We are always one second away from sin and thank God, His forgiveness is immediately available.

Remember when I talked about sins of the heart and how I need to guard my heart. Confession and forgiveness are protectors of my heart. They are protectors of your heart.

Chapter 24

Confession of Sin

Every morning, I come before the Lord's throne of mercy and grace asking for forgiveness and asking God for a heart to forgive others. God and I do not necessarily go through a list of sin (though that is necessary some days), but rather it is a time for confessing that I am a sinner in need of God's forgiveness and how in Christ I need to be forgiving.

Confession keeps my focus on God and the finished work of Christ. To be honest, the daily confession keeps me humble. It's a reminder that my worth is in Christ. Self takes a back seat to Christ.

I just had a new thought about the importance of confession. I have always thought of confession as the admission of sin. However, confession is also an admission of forgiveness. Our confession is that we are sinners who can claim God's forgiveness in Christ. (You just took a step with me as God walks with me. This is how God's walk with us works; He gives us little insights each day as He walks with us. I enjoyed sharing this step with you.)

Look at 1 John 1:8, 9 with me again: "If we confess our sins" then "He is faithful and righteous to forgive us our sins." Confession of sin comes first and forgiveness follows. I believe all our sins, past, present and future, have already been forgiven. However, I believe it takes the confession of those sins before we can experience God's healing power of forgiveness in Christ.

Confession is not a works in God's walks with us. It is a necessary part of any relationship that hopes to be strong and full of love and commitment. We need to receive forgiveness. We need to give forgiveness. Confession of sin is an important step toward forgiveness in God's walk with us. Confession of God's forgiveness is another important step.

True confession involves us agreeing with God in our hearts that we have committed sin. Confession is not just a verbal assertion. It is not just apologizing because God believes it is wrong. It is confessing sin from our hearts. It takes Christ in our hearts to truly confess our sins.

Our sinful nature wants to defend us and deflect the guilt for our sin. Look at Adam and Eve, the first to sin. Eve blamed it on the serpent and Adam blamed it on Eve. God put the guilt for their choices on them. We are guilty of our choices.

This heart felt confession is married to repentance. Remember what Christ told the woman caught in adultery (the woman other sinners wanted to stone), Christ told her to sin no more. God's forgiveness included the command to sin no more. Our confession involves a desire to repent from the sin and commit it no more. Repentance is another important step in the forgiveness process.

John the Baptist's role in the kingdom of God was to prepare Israel for the coming of its messiah. What was John the Baptist's message? His message was Matthew 3:2:

> "Repent, for the kingdom of heaven is at hand."

Repent from what? Repent from our sin. To be able to repent from sin, you need to confess it as sin.

Chapter 25

Confession of God's Forgiveness

John the Baptist's message was the repentance from sin. If God's message ended there we would have no hope. Fortunately for us, God's message didn't end there and we have forgiveness in Christ.

There still may be consequences in our lives from our sin but the penalty has been paid. The consequences we may endure are not a payment for our sin; Christ's finished work is the payment.

God has provided a biblical example of just how forgivable we are in Christ through the story of King David's sins. King David's sins have probably received more attention than anyone else's; maybe because God gives it so much attention.

The story starts in 2 Samuel 11. David was home and had not gone to war with his army. The way the verse is written (2 Samuel 11:1), David would have been expected to go to war with his army; but he didn't. We don't know why he didn't go, but him not going may have been his first sin; he may not have been occupied with the work the Lord had given him.

David couldn't sleep, so he goes for a walk on his rooftop (I say he can't sleep because 2 Samuel 11:2 says he arose from his bed). From his rooftop he sees Bathsheba and he is infatuated and inquires of her identity. He wants to know who this beautiful woman is that he saw. He learns that she is the wife of Uriah, one of his trusted soldiers and friend. That should have been reason enough to flee the temptation as Joseph did.

Well, David didn't resist and he lusted in his heart (sin number 2). He had to have her; never mind that she is married and married to one of his friends. He sends for Bathsheba and he sleeps with her (sin number 3). Remember, though, he committed the sin in his heart before he committed it in his bed.

There is just one unforeseen complication; she gets pregnant. Now I understand, from what we read, that David only slept with her once. His lust was satisfied. But once was enough to get her pregnant and now there is a problem; David's sin can be discovered.

So what does David do? He sends for Uriah in hopes that he will sleep with his wife and no one will be the wiser. He will hide his sin; quick thinking.

The problem is that Uriah is a rather righteous person who has a problem with sleeping with his wife (see 2 Samuel 11:11) while the army is still at war. David tries to get him drunk so he will be less aware of his righteous position; does not work.

So David moves on to Plan B; sin number 4. He sends Uriah back to the war with a note for Joab, the commander of the army. 2 Samuel 11:15 tells us what was in the note:

> "And he had written in the letter, saying, "Place Uriah in the front line of the fiercest battle and withdraw from him, so that he may be struck down and die.""

David ordered his death. And then, after awaiting the appropriate amount of time after his death, he marries Bathsheba.

David, however, forgot something very important while he was engaging in all these sins. 2 Samuel 11:27 tells us:

> "But the thing that David had done was evil in the sight of the Lord."

God saw David's sins. David had turned away from God while he was sinning. God, however, had not turned away from David. Nathan confronts David and here is the beauty of the whole story as found in 2 Samuel 12:13:

> "Then David said to Nathan, "I have sinned against the Lord." And Nathan said to David, "The Lord also has taken away your sin; you shall not die.""

David confesses his sin. God forgives David. What a beautiful testimony of God's commitment to forgive.

However, the story doesn't end there. There was a consequence for David's sins. The child borne to David and Bathsheba dies. A son dies as a result of another's sin. It's interesting to me that the son died. Was it a foretelling of the death of the Son of God to save us from sin?

And yet, the story still hasn't ended. David and Bathsheba have a second son, Solomon. Yes, King Solomon, who is listed in the lineage of Christ, is the son of David and Bathsheba. Let's read what it says in Matthew 1:6:

> "And to David was born Solomon by her who had been the wife of Uriah;"

To me it is just fascinating how Solomon is the son of David and Bathsheba, a relationship that started with the adulterous sin of David. God did forgive David and Bathsheba. He allowed their son to be the next king and part of the lineage of Christ.

Just as David confessed his sin, we must confess our sin. And just as God forgave David, He forgives us. He has forgiven us if we have placed our faith in Christ's finished work. The real issue isn't whether or not we are forgiven. We are forgiven. The issue is whether or not we are experiencing the forgiveness we have in Christ.

To experience forgiveness, we need to agree with God about our sin. We need to agree with God about our forgiveness. Confessing the sin without claiming God's forgiveness does not heal us. The claiming of the forgiveness is part of the healing. Sin creates a wound in our relationship with God; forgiveness heals the wound.

Luke 24:46-48 records Christ's request to his disciples and followers:

> "and He said to them, 'Thus it is written, that the Christ should suffer and rise again from the dead the third day; and that repentance for forgiveness of sins should be proclaimed in His name to all the nations, beginning from Jerusalem. You are the witnesses of these things."

Our confession of God's forgiveness of our sins is a proclamation to the nations of the finished work of Christ. Our confession is a witness of Christ's finished work. We need the confession for our lives and others need our confession for their lives. Our confession of forgiveness heals us, encourages other believers in God's walks with them and leads non-believers to faith in Christ.

Chapter 26

Forgiveness of Ourselves

I think for most of us, the hardest person to forgive is ourselves. We commit certain sins and wonder how God could ever forgive us because we see ourselves as unforgivable. We are not unforgiveable in God's eyes, we are unforgiveable in our own eyes. For some reason we can't seem to forgive ourselves.

I want to begin with this thought: If God has forgiven you, how can you not forgive yourself? Is your struggle to forgive yourself really because you are unforgiveable or is it because you can't do anything to warrant the forgiveness?

God's forgiveness is not warranted on our works but on Christ's finished work. You need to confess the forgiveness you have in Christ. Then and only then, will you find the forgiveness you seek for yourself.

Now, understand, you may need to do something to correct the harm you have caused as a result of your sin. However, this action results from the forgiveness you already have received in Christ, it does not earn your forgiveness.

Ephesians 1:7-8 says it so well. I encourage you to memorize these verses.

> "In Him we have redemption through His blood, the forgiveness of our trespasses, according to the riches of His grace, which He lavished upon us."

Forgiveness is a gift of grace that God freely gives. If you ask God, He will give you the ability to forgive yourself. He does not want you to suffer in guilt but rather feel the healing power of forgiveness.

Nothing is gained by not forgiving ourselves. It does not solve the problem of our sin and does not bring healing to ourselves or others.

We are sinners. That has not changed. You will sin again. I will sin again. And God will forgive us again. We need to rest in God's forgiveness for our own forgiveness.

When we don't forgive ourselves, after God has forgiven us, we take our eyes off of God and put them on ourselves. Christ is no longer Lord of our lives but our sense of self becomes our focus. Beware of the self-righteousness of guilt. It will not save you and it will interfere with your relationship with God and others.

Chapter 27

Forgiveness of Others

BESIDES NEEDING TO FORGIVE OURSELVES, WE NEED OTHERS TO forgive us. Our sin can have an impact on others and we need to be willing to confess our sin to them and ask their forgiveness.

When we confess our sins to others we cannot control their responses. They may forgive us; they may not. Our responsibility in Christ is to confess and ask for the forgiveness.

When we ask for the forgiveness, we need to respect the other person's need to work through their forgiveness. The deeper the wound, the longer it takes to heal. Remember that it caused God great pain to forgive us; Christ had to die on a cross. People need to work through the pain to forgive us. Our sin can be quite hurtful.

The other person may not want to forgive you and you cannot demand that they do. Others forgiveness of us is between them and God. You may be sincere in your confession but that does not mean the person is able to forgive or will forgive.

We confess as part of our healing process. We confess as part of their healing process and because we want their forgiveness. We do not confess so they have to forgive us. They don't have to forgive us. We confess because it is the right thing to do in Christ.

We also need to forgive others who have sinned against us. We need to forgive even if they do not feel the need for our forgiveness.

This morning in my devotional I read Matthew 18:21-35. The first two verses, Matthew 18:21, 22 deal with how often we should forgive someone:

> "Then Peter came and said to Him, "Lord, how often shall my brother sin against me and I forgive him? Up to seven times?" Jesus said to him, "I do not say to you, up to seven times, but up to seventy times seven.""

Right after that statement, He tells the story of a king who wants to receive payment from some of his servants for their outstanding debts. A servant who owes the king a very large sum of money requests mercy and the king forgives his debt.

This same servant then meets up with a fellow servant who owes him money. The sum is very small compared to what the king just forgave this one servant. Again, mercy is requested. However, this time mercy was not given.

The king learns of this servant's unwillingness to forgive the debt of his fellow servant and says in Matthew 18:33:

> "Should you not also have had mercy on your fellow slave, even as I had mercy on you?"

Jesus closes the story with Matthew 18:35:

> "So shall My heavenly Father also do to you, if each of you does not forgive his brother from your heart."

Forgiveness is very important in our relationship with God and our relationship with others. We need to confess the forgiveness we have in Christ as we interact with each other and we need to forgive one another. People need to feel forgiven.

We are to forgive as Christ has forgiven us. We forgive because as God walks with us forgiveness becomes a part of who we are in Christ. His forgiving heart becomes our forgiving heart.

We forgive because we need to heal. Forgiveness is this wonderful tool that God uses in our lives to cleanse our hearts. It is to our hearts what soap is to our bodies.

I close this chapter with Ephesians 4:32 which says:

> "And be kind to one another, tender-hearted, forgiving each other, just as God in Christ also has forgiven you."

Chapter 28

Healing Power

FORGIVENESS HAS A VERY HEALING EFFECT ON OUR LIVES. I believe a lot of broken relationships could be healed, if people could forgive and be forgiven. I thank God that I have forgiveness in Christ and can have a relationship with the God of the universe.

God has used forgiveness to bring a lot of healing to my heart. Wounds of childhood carry into adulthood and interfere with who we can be. Through forgiveness God has allowed me to grow past the wounds. His love defines me, rather than the wounds.

Sin does wound us. I have never met someone who has not been wounded by the sin of another. But forgiveness heals the wounds. I encourage people to forgive so they can heal. Forgiveness might be the purest form of love. I Peter 4:8 says:

> "Above all, keep fervent in your love for one another, because love covers a multitude of sins."

God loves us, thus, we can love others. God forgives us, thus, we can forgive others. God's forgiveness heals us and our forgiveness heals us and others.

To heal someone is to make them healthy or well again. God's forgiveness makes our relationship with Him healthy again. Rather than being dead in sin we are alive in Christ.

Forgiveness can make our relationships with others healthy again. Doesn't it feel good when someone says I'm sorry? The apology touches something deep within us that says we matter. That's important.

I have forgiven others and it has not healed our relationship. In most cases, it is because the other does not feel the need for the forgiveness. In other cases, it is because the person really hasn't repented; the person does not feel the need to be forgiven.

I am still healed because I forgave. The other's healing is dependent on that person. And, unfortunately, sometimes sin changes a relationship even after forgiveness. There are consequences for our sin.

However, healing is still a reality even if the relationship changes. Even the body after certain injuries is not the same. Our hearts and our relationships are not always the same after some injuries.

But just as the body can heal so can our hearts. Forgiveness is the power for healing our heart relationship with God and each other.

Chapter 29

Closing Thoughts

I HAVE HAD TO FORGIVE PEOPLE WHO HAVE NOT YET CONFESSED how they sinned against me and probably never will. They probably don't even believe they have sinned against me.

Do they experience my forgiveness? No.

Do I experience my forgiveness? Yes. God has healed me of the wounds of their sin. And, part of the healing process was for me to forgive.

Do you want more joy in your life and not bitterness? Forgive.

Do you want more peace in your life and not strife? Forgive.

Do you want more love in your life and not hatred? Forgive.

Forgiveness has the power to heal, but it must be exercised. It is not enough to give lip service. You must forgive from the heart.

For me, it starts at the throne of mercy and grace of our forgiving God. In Christ, I am forgiven and so I can have a heart that can forgive. It is not I who forgives, it is the Spirit of Christ within me that gives me the power to forgive and to heal.

If I was to encourage next steps for you, it would be to first confess God's forgiveness of you. A confession that heals you and fills you with His unconditional love.

Next, claim your own forgiveness of self through the forgiveness you have in Christ. Only after you have experienced God's forgiveness and your own forgiveness can you freely forgive others who have sinned against you and freely accept the forgiveness of others.

Finally, forgive those you believe have sinned against you. Ask God to fill your heart with forgiveness.

I remember one time when I had to forgive someone who had caused me much pain. I thought I had forgiven him until God asked me to pray for him. Forgiveness was one thing, praying for him was another matter. I learned that I can only pray for someone if I have truly forgiven them. So, pray for those who need your forgiveness.

God has freely forgiven us in Christ and He wants us to do the same for each other. I close with Colossians 3:12, 13:

> "And so, as those who have been chosen of God, holy and beloved, put on a heart of compassion, kindness, humility, gentleness and patience; bearing with one another, and forgiving each other, whoever has a complaint against anyone; just as the Lord forgave you, so also should you."

Christ in Us

"Now the Lord is the Spirit; and where the Spirit of the Lord is there is liberty (2 Corinthians 3:17)."

Chapter 30

Introduction

CHRIST IN US IS VERY REAL. AND YET, I BELIEVE IT IS A DIFFICULT concept for us to comprehend. How does it work to have Christ in us? Does He somehow 'possess' us? Do we feel Him in us? Do we feel different?

In this truth, we will discuss what it means to have Christ in us, in other words, to have the power of God through the Holy Spirit at work in us and through us.

When we discussed the Reality of Sin, there were two aspects to it; there was the sin we commit and there was the power of sin that resides in us. During our discussion of the truth, Forgiveness Heals, we addressed the forgiveness of the sins we commit. When we discuss Christ in Us we will address the power He gives us over the power of sin through His Spirit who resides in us.

Hopefully, when we are done, you will have a better understanding of the battle within you between the presence of the power of sin and the presence of the power of the Holy Spirit (the Spirit of Christ). They are both present in you as a believer. And, they both want control of your choices.

The former for its own desires and the latter to accomplish God's perfect will for you. I believe this struggle is the true test of one's faith in the finished work of Christ.

One day I was driving to work and I was exhausted. I remember telling God that I would be on auto-pilot for the day. Instantly, I knew I had it wrong. Self would not be the pilot but Christ through the Holy Spirit would pilot me through the day.

As I thought about the concept of auto-pilot I thought about the piloting of an airplane and I realized that it made a great analogy. There are three basic pilots for the plane. You have the human pilot. You have auto-pilot which means the airplane itself is its pilot. And you have other possibilities piloting the plane like turbulent weather. The airplane at any one time can only have one pilot.

As Christians, the principle is the same. Our lives can only have one pilot. It will be Christ or it will be us or it will be something or someone else. And while the plane does not have a choice, the pilot of our lives is our choice.

Taking this analogy a bit further. An airplane is an airplane regardless of the pilot. The pilot determines how well the airplane flies, he does not change the fact that it is still an airplane.

The same is true for us. When Christ is our pilot; we don't stop being us. I am a better me when Christ is in control and He works through me. However, I don't cease to exist because God is in control. The difference is who is in control of my choices: God or "I."

So, when you think of your life, think of who is in control of your choices. Are you allowing Christ to pilot you or are you piloting you or are you allowing something or someone else to pilot you?

Someone or something is in control of the choices we make. Whether it be us or we give the control to another. As Christians, hopefully, we have given Christ control of our choices.

I like what Joshua states it in Joshua 24:15:

> "And if it is disagreeable in your sight to serve the Lord, choose for yourselves today whom you will serve: whether the gods which your fathers served which were beyond the River, or the gods of the Amorites in whose land you are living; but as for me and my house, we will serve the Lord."

I say along with Joshua that I will serve the Lord and have Him pilot my life. Matthew 6:24 expounds on this idea:

> "No one can serve two masters; for either he will hate the one and love the other, or he will hold to one and despise the other. You cannot serve God and mammon."

Jesus promised His disciples, and thus us, His power to live out God's walk with us. He told His disciples in Luke 24:49:

> "And behold, I am sending forth the promise of My Father upon you; but you are to stay in the city until you are clothed with power from on high."

Christ's promise of power was fulfilled in Acts 2:1-4:

> "And when the day of Pentecost had come, they were all together in one place. And suddenly there came from heaven a noise like a violent, rushing wind, and it filled the whole house where they were sitting. And there appeared to them tongues as of fire distributing themselves, and they rested on each one of them. And there were all filled with the Holy Spirit..."

Christ does not somehow possess us but rather works with us and through us. I can't say I feel Him in me but I can say I am often surprised by how I handle things and know that it had to be Christ in me.

He is in us through the Holy Spirit being in us. He is in us because he made a promise in Matthew 28:20:

> "and lo, I am with you always, even to the end of the age."

I do believe we feel different. We feel God's forgiveness, love and acceptance. We have a new sense of us because of Christ's finished work for us. We have assurance of salvation. We can face the challenges of life because He walks with us!

Chapter 31

Our Triune God

As Christians we often talk about our triune God or the Trinity. As a Catholic, I would do the sign of the cross and say, "Father, Son and Holy Ghost." Basically, by being a triune God, God has revealed Himself to us through three roles.

The first role through which He was made Himself known to us is as the role of God. In the Old Testament, He was just God. Exodus 3: 13, 14 provides an exchange between Moses and God that illustrates this point:

> "Then Moses said to God, 'Behold, I am going to the sons of Israel, and I shall say to them, 'The God of your fathers has sent me to you.' Now they may say to me, 'What is His name?' What shall I say to them?' And God said to Moses, 'I AM WHO I AM;' and He said, 'Thus you shall say to the sons of Israel, 'I AM has sent me to you.'''"

In the New Testament we are introduced to God as our Father. The Lord's Prayer in Matthew 6:9-13 begins:

> "Our Father who art in heaven."

The second role through which He has revealed Himself to us is through His actions as the Spirit of God. In the Old Testament, we see actions of the Spirit of God in creation and coming upon people for whom God had a special purpose or work. In the New Testament, the Spirit of God is often referred to as the Holy Spirit or the Spirit of Christ. We will discuss this role in the next chapter.

And, the third role through which He has made Himself known to us is through the Son of God, Jesus Christ. In the Old Testament, believers in faith looked forward to His finished work. In the New Testament, we look back at His finished work.

It is not three gods, but three roles through which the one and only true God has chosen to reveal Himself to us. God the Father and the Son of God we can somehow picture because we associate physical pictures to the roles. The Spirit of God is more difficult because there is not a physical picture. And yet, it is probably the truer picture of God's existence.

John tells us in John 1:18:

> "No man has seen God at any time; the only begotten God, who is in the bosom of the Father, He has explained Him."

The only begotten is Jesus Christ. We don't know what God looks like. We don't know in what form He exists.

We do know that He has revealed Himself through His Word, the Bible, and through His Son, Jesus Christ. We also know that He has given us His Spirit that we might know Him better.

God is above our physical world and yet we are confined to our words to try to explain Him. As I read the Bible, I do not see where the writers felt a need to explain how God revealed Himself. God's existence was accepted. How God revealed Himself was accepted. The first commandment found in Exodus 20:3 states,

> "You shall have no other gods before Me."

In a later commandment He states, "for I, the Lord your God." God makes it clear He is the one and only God.

I believe we need to accept Him and His revelations of Himself by faith. That does not mean we should not study His Word to better know Him and His revealed roles, but I do think that we will be limited in our understanding as long as we are in these bodies.

Paul says it well in 1 Corinthians 13:12:

> "For now we see in a mirror dimly, but then face to face; now I know in part, but then I shall know fully just as I also have been fully known."

Chapter 32

The Holy Spirit

We often think of the Holy Spirit as a New Testament phenomenon and as a result of Christ's finished work. However, the Spirit of God was very active in the creation of the world and the lives of people in the Old Testament chosen by God for works He purposed for them.

The first mention of the Holy Spirit defines that He is the Spirit of God. We first read of Him in His role in creation. Let's read Genesis 1:2:

> "And the earth was formless and void, and darkness was over the surface of the deep; and the Spirit of God was moving over the surface of the waters."

Throughout the Old Testament we see the Spirit of God working through people. These people had various job descriptions and God worked through those job descriptions. He prepared them for the work He purposed for them and He equipped them for the work.

In Exodus 31:3, the Spirit of God works through an artisan:

> "And I have filled him with the Spirit of God in wisdom, in understanding, in knowledge, and in all kinds of craftsmanship,"

He works through the seventy to share Moses' burden for judging the people in Numbers 11:16, 17:

> "The Lord therefore said to Moses, "Gather for Me seventy men from the elders of Israel, whom you know to be the elders of the people and their officers and bring them to the tent of meeting, and let them take their stand there with you. Then I will come down and speak with you there, and I will take of the Spirit who is upon you, and will put Him upon them; and they shall bear the burden of the people with you, so that you shall not bear it all alone."

We see Him active in the life of Judge Othniel in Judges 3:10:

> "And the Spirit of the Lord came upon him, and he judged Israel."

God tells the prophet Samuel in 1 Samuel 10:6:

> "Then the Spirit of the Lord will come upon you mightily..."

And, as our last example, in 1 Samuel 16:13 we see the Spirit of the Lord descending on David:

> "and the Spirit of the Lord came mightily upon David from that day forward."

If we look closer at these lives we won't see perfect people. We won't see something about them that set them apart from other people except that the hand of God had chosen them. God could have chosen others, but He chose them. The Old and New Testaments are filled of examples of God using people to accomplish His will.

Also, note that God called them for that work for which He had already prepared them and was preparing them. The artisan was already gifted for the work "in all kinds of craftsmanship." Samuel was set aside from an early age and knew at the appointed time that "the Spirit of the Lord" would come upon him "mightily."

And, David as a shepherd learned to lead and care for a flock. David also spent years learning to lead men and wage war before he ever became king.

For all these men, it was a process that brought them to their place of calling in God's plan. And the Holy Spirit was part of that process.

As believers, we have that same Holy Spirit to equip us for the work that God has purposed for us. We have that same power working in us to accomplish God's plan for us. We have God walking with us.

My goal, however, with this truth is not talk to about the process by which God works in and through us, but to talk about the presence of the Holy Spirit in our lives to overcome the power of sin.

Chapter 33

Power Over Sin

IN CHAPTER 21, WE LOOKED CLOSELY AT ROMANS 7 AND THE struggle between the desire for the believer to fulfill the law of God and the desire of the flesh to sin. Romans 7 closes with these great verses, Romans 7:24, 25:

> "Wretched man that I am! Who will set me free from the body of this death? Thanks be to God through Jesus Christ our Lord! So then, on the one hand I myself with my mind am serving the law of God, but on the other, with my flesh the law of sin."

There is a solution to the power of sin in our lives. But please note, the struggle will always be there. The Apostle Paul, the author of the Book of Romans, does not say that the flesh no longer serves sin, but that with his mind he can serve the law of God.

There is victory in this struggle we have with the power of sin. The Apostle Paul tells us that it is through Jesus Christ. Romans 8 describes that victory. Praise God for Romans 8. Let's start with Romans 8:1-4:

> "There is therefore now no condemnation for those who are in Christ Jesus. For the law of the Spirit of life in Christ Jesus has set you free from the law of sin, and of death. For what the Law could not do, weak as it was through the flesh, God did: sending His own Son in the likeness of sinful flesh and as an offering for sin, He condemned sin in the flesh, in order that the requirements of the Law might be fulfilled in us, who do not walk according to the flesh, but according to the Spirit."

The solution to the power of sin in our lives is walking "according to the Spirit." Walking is something you do one step at a time. Let's continue with Romans 8:9-11:

> "However, you are not it the flesh but in the Spirit, if indeed the Spirit of God dwells in you. But if anyone does not have the Spirit of Christ, he does not belong to Him. And if Christ is in you, though the body is dead because of sin, yet the spirit is alive because of righteousness. But if the Spirit of Him who raised Jesus from the dead dwells in you, He who raised Christ Jesus from the dead will also give life to your mortal bodies through His Spirit who indwells you."

The Apostle Paul is establishing that what he is saying only applies to people who have placed their faith in Christ (Saving Faith). If you have placed your faith in Christ, then you have the Spirit of Christ (the Holy Spirit).

For those of us in Christ, the flesh has lost the war. We still have the battles with the flesh, but in the Spirit we will be victorious in living the life we have in Christ. It is a wonderful promise.

Yet, we still sin. We still sin because we are still in this body. We will lose some battles with sin, but the war has been won. Paul tells us in Romans 8:12-14:

> "So then, brethren, we are under obligation, not to the flesh; to live according to the flesh - for if you are living according to the flesh, you must die; but if by the Spirit you are putting to death the deeds of the body, you will live. For all who are being led by the Spirit of God, these are sons of God."

By the Spirit we are "putting to death the deeds of the body." Putting is active and continual; it is not in the past but a continual act in our daily lives. Through the power of the Holy Spirit in us we are daily putting to death the deeds of the body which are sinful.

Herein, I believe, lies the problem for many of us; we forget that it is a daily battle. Yes, Christ has won the war for us but as long as we are in these bodies there will be the battle between our sinful nature and our faith in Christ. It is the reality of the Christian. In Christ, we are engaged in the battle knowing that our victory is in Christ. We are learning what Paul said in Galatians 2:20:

> "I have been crucified with Christ; and it is no longer I who live, but Christ lives in me; and the life which I now live in the flesh I live by faith in the Son of God, who loved me, and delivered Himself up for me."

There are no formulas for God's walk with us unless it is the formula of faith. I am an engineer and so I am trained to define a problem and select the appropriate formula for the solution of the problem. We have the problem of sin. The appropriate formula is faith in Christ Who is in us. The battles are won by trusting the power of the Holy Spirit in us to win.

It is a daily choice to apply faith in Christ to our lives. Actually, since we are always one second away from sin, it is a continual choice to apply faith in Christ to our lives. Fortunately, Christ is in us through the Holy Spirit to continually empower us in that choice.

Christ is not a second away but always present walking with us through the battles. But like a baby, we first learn to crawl before we walk. In other words, we learn to trust in the power of God in our lives. It is a lifelong process.

This lifelong process is what I believe Peter meant when he wrote in 1 Peter 2:1, 2:

> "Therefore, putting aside all malice and all guile and hypocrisy, and envy and all slander, like newborn babes, long for the pure milk of the word, that by it you may grow in respect to salvation."

We grow in our relationship to our salvation through the finished work in Christ. Our life in Christ is a lifelong walk with the Spirit of Christ present in us to give us victory. We don't wake up one morning and we have arrived.

Earlier Peter wrote in 1 Peter 1:13:

> "Therefore, gird your minds for action, keep sober in spirit, fix your hope completely on the grace to be brought to you at the revelation of Jesus Christ."

Our life in Christ begins with us submitting to the Spirit of Christ in us. Our life in Christ continues by letting the Spirit of Christ pilot our lives. We don't stop being us. We just learn, through the Spirit, to resist the sins of the flesh as He walks with us.

If you have every watched a baby learn to walk, you will see that they stumble and fall. And what does every loving parent do, they pick up the baby, comfort the baby, and encourage the baby to walk again. Actually, they take the baby by the hand and walk with him/her.

God does the same with us. Just as the loving parent holds the hand of his child as they walk together, our loving Father is holding our hand as He walks with us.

Chapter 34

Closing Thoughts

We will stumble and fall as we learn what it means to have Him walk with us. God has given us His Holy Spirit to empower us for the walk. I do not marvel that I stumble. I marvel that God forgives me each time and takes me by the hand and says let's keep walking together.

I encourage you to take steps of faith and trust in the Spirit of God in you. It is by faith that we learn to trust the power of the Holy Spirit in us to face the battles each day. And each day, He is found faithful.

By faith, let Him pilot you through your life. There will be turbulence, but who better to manage the turbulence than Christ in you.

God has been walking with me for over 30 years now and I still have to ask each day that the Holy Spirit lead me and keep me. I pray the Lord's Prayer pretty much every day and I always think about Matthew 6:13 which reads,

> "And do not lead us into temptation, but deliver us from evil."

As I pray through the prayer, I thank the Lord that He does not lead me into temptation and does keep me from evil. Because the verse begins with the idea of temptation, I think of delivering us from evil as keeping me from committing the sin that is tempting me. Temptation will come in our lives, what we need is the power to resist and not commit evil by sinning.

There is evil in the world from which God does deliver us. I often think of that trip when the owner of the mechanic's shop wanted to harm me. God delivered me from his evil intent.

However, there is also evil that we will endure because people are sinners and we are His children. For me, the prayer is that I will not commit evil as a result of the temptation or as a result of the sin of others toward me. I think of the prayer as asking God to deliver me from committing evil.

God, through His Holy Spirit, does provide the power to resist temptation and not sin, and to endure the evil of the sin of others and forgive. We need to learn to trust His power working in and through us. It is a trust that grows each day as He walks with us.

Is there sin in your life that you need to trust the power of God to overcome? The sin may not just be actions but emotions and/or attitudes. Today, and every day, consider "putting" the sin aside and trusting the power of God for new choices.

Remember, it starts with baby steps. Let's take baby steps of faith today and trust that God will give us the power to overcome. God will give you the power to overcome as He walks with you.

I close with 1 John 5:4, 5:

> "For whatever is born of God overcomes the world; and this is the victory that has overcome the world – our faith. And who is the one who overcomes the world, but he who believes that Jesus is the Son of God?"

Faith

"I have been young and now I am old; Yet I have not seen the righteous forsaken (Psalms 37:25)."

Chapter 35

Introduction

When we have faith in someone or something, it is because we trust them to perform as promised. We believe that the promised actions will be accomplished. We have confidence in the ability of the person or thing to perform.

Everybody believes in someone or something. The question we all need to ask ourselves is if that in which we believe is worthy of our trust and confidence; is worthy of our faith.

I believe the God of the Bible is worthy of my faith. I believe in the finished work of Christ. I believe the Holy Spirit is active in my life making me more like Christ. I have faith that He walks with me.

My faith is based on the trustworthiness of God's Word, the Bible, and supporting evidence in my life and the lives of others of God's faithfulness. God still gives me hugs when I need them. He actually has done so much more than merely given me hugs.

I truly believe God has given me the faith to believe and continually proves His faithfulness to me. It is an interesting paradigm; we need the faith only God can give us, and without faith it is impossible to please Him.

I think what often happens within us is that we fear what is to come and even though we know we should trust God, we look for someone or something we can see and touch to trust. It's almost like we say that we trust God, but meanwhile put plan B in action. It is times like these that I say as the father in Mark 9:24 said,

> "I do believe; help my unbelief."

The supporting evidence of our faith in Christ is God's walk with us in Christ. If we believe in Christ's finished work there will be evidence of the Holy Spirit working in us. As Romans 8:4 says:

> "in order that the requirements of the Law might be fulfilled in us, who do not walk according to the flesh, but according to the Spirit."

For the fun of it I looked up the definition of walk which is to move with your legs slower than running. It just told me what it is not. It is not running. And then, of course, you have leisure walks, power walks, and a walk in basketball, police walk a beat, etc.

So, what is a walk? I believe a walk is putting one foot in front of the other with the intent of getting somewhere or accomplishing something. Our faith walk in Christ has the intent of us becoming more like Christ.

Psalms 119:105 tells us:

> "Thy word is a lamp to my feet. And a light to my path."

When you put a lamp at your feet it sheds enough light for the next step. When, by faith, we believe God walks with us, it is often with only knowing the next step He has for us to take. God walks with us one step at a time. And His word, the Bible, is the light to our path.

Chapter 36

Biblical Faith

Hebrews 11 is the chapter on faith. It has been called the Hall of Fame for Old Testament believers. It opens by providing the definition of faith. Let's read Hebrews 11:1, 2:

> "Now faith is the assurance of things hoped for, the conviction of things not seen. For by it the men of old gained approval."

That is a great definition for faith. It is complete. Three key words stand out for me; assurance, hope and conviction. I would love to do a chapter on each of the three.

The other important truth about this definition is that it is how men of old gained approval. We often talk about them for their works, but for God it was their faith. And for God, it is our faith. We gain God's approval by our faith and not our works. I should say by faith in Christ and His finished work we gain God's approval. Hebrews 11:6 goes on to say:

> "And without faith it is impossible to please Him, for he who comes to God must believe that He is, and that He is a rewarder of those who seek Him."

God is more interested in our faith in Him than our works for Him. Our works will come as a result of our faith. Our faith will not come as a result of our works. It's significant that God says that we must believe that 'He is' and that 'He is a rewarder of those who seek Him.' He will reward our seeking. Our faith pleases Him.

We often try to work out our faith rather than let our faith work. Before I say more, let's read Hebrews 12:1, 2 together:

> "Therefore, since we have so great a cloud of witnesses surrounding us, let us also lay aside every encumbrance, and the sin which so easily entangles us, and let us run with endurance the race that is set before us, fixing our eyes on Jesus, the author and perfecter of faith, who for the joy set before Him endured the cross, despising the shame, and has sat down at the right hand of the throne of God."

The cloud of witnesses is everyone that was just listed in Hebrews 11. A witness testifies of what he knows. What is the testimony of these witnesses? Their testimony is their faith in God and His faithfulness to them.

Just as they had faith, we are to have faith and lay aside those things that get in the way of experiencing God walking with us. Notice it says to lay aside that sin "which so easily entangles us." It is an act of faith to set sin aside. It is an act of faith in the healing power of forgiveness and the power of the Holy Spirit in our lives to set sin aside. Also note, sin comes easy to us.

And after we set it aside, we are to "run with endurance the race that is set before us." I Corinthians 9:24-27 sheds some light on the race:

> "Do you not know that those who run in a race all run, but only one receives the prize? Run in such a way that you may win. And everyone who competes in the games exercises self-control in all things. They then do it to receive a perishable wreath, but we an imperishable. Therefore I run in such a way, as not without aim; I box in such a way, as not beating the air; but I buffet my body and make it my slave, lest possibly after I have preached to others, I myself should be disqualified."

The race symbolizes someone who is trained to compete with the goal of winning the prize. For the believer, the prize is found in Philippians 3:14:

> "I press on toward the goal for the prize of the upward call of God in Christ Jesus."

Our prize is our relationship in Christ. What an awesome prize.

Hebrews 12:1, 2 continues by telling us to run the race by "fixing our eyes on Jesus, the author and perfecter of faith." We don't fix our eyes on ourselves or others or even on our own faith. We fix on eyes on Jesus who is the "author and perfecter of faith."

You want to grow in faith? Fix your eyes on Jesus and His finished work and the word of God. His finished work is the proof of why He is the "author and perfecter of faith."

It is through Christ, through His Spirit in us, that we have faith and can run the race. It is through the Holy Spirit working in us that we grow in faith in Christ. An athlete doesn't wake up one morning and run a marathon; rather he trains for it. We need training for our faith.

Christ is our trainer through His Spirit who is in us. He uses circumstances in our lives to build our faith in Him. Matthew 11:29 tells us:

> "Take My yoke upon you, and learn from Me, for I am gentle and humble in heart; and you shall find rest for your souls."

I like when Scripture just comes together so nicely. Christ is the author and perfecter of our faith by yoking Himself to us. He teaches us in the walk of faith and our souls find rest in Him. My experience, as God walks with me, is that I do find peace when I, in faith, rest in Him.

In 1 Corinthians 9:24-27, Paul also speaks about an athlete buffeting his/her body and making it his slave. He is making the comparison that we must buffet our hearts and not give sin a chance to again gain power over us.

We gain power over sin by taking His yoke upon us. We do this by giving the piloting of our lives over to the Holy Spirit who is in us. We do this by keeping our eyes fixed on Christ and the prize of "the upward call of God in Christ Jesus." And we do it all by faith!

Chapter 37

Walking in Faith

I JUST LIKE THE CONCEPT THAT OUR RELATIONSHIP WITH THE Lord is like taking a walk. It assumes movement. It assumes companionship. It assumes progress. It assumes a relationship that involves the enjoyment of each other's company.

God wants a relationship with us. God wants a relationship with me. God wants a relationship with you. God wants to walk with us.

But the walk is only a symbol of the process by which we become more like Christ. As a child grows, he/she learns more about his/her role in our physical world. He/she learns how to relate to others, how to be involved in the larger society, how to become a responsible adult and how to, hopefully, help others. The child crawls and then the child walks.

In our Christian lives we must grow in our understanding of our place in God's world. We crawl and then we walk. Christ is our Teacher. The Holy Spirit is our source of strength. He walks with us. Again looking at what Christ says in Matthew 11:29, 30:

> "Take My yoke upon you, and learn from Me, for I am gentle and humble in heart; and you will find

> rest for your souls. For My yoke is easy, and My load is light."

A yoke is the tool that is used to tie oxen together so they work as one. If you had an inexperienced ox, it would be yoked to a more experienced ox. The more experienced ox than teaches and helps train the less experienced.

Christ is saying that through the Holy Spirit we will be yoked to Him. He will teach and train us. And, He will do it with gentleness and humility. We often fear God's training and yet, Christ makes it clear that we will find rest for our souls.

If you have ever seen oxen working together it is usually in a walk mode. They walk sharing the load. Christ is saying that He is walking with us and that He is sharing the load. He has given us the Holy Spirit to strengthen us in Him. Truth be known, He actually carries the whole load and yet we are a part of it.

The walk is taken one step at a time; one step at a time by faith in Christ. The problem we have as Christians is that we so want to tell God that we are good and He can trust us. He can worry about someone else. But apart from Christ we are nothing.

It is only in Christ, in our yoke in Christ, that we are anything before God. It is not God's purpose to make us more so we don't need Him, but to make Christ more in us. Paul says it so well in Galatians 2:20:

> "I have been crucified with Christ; and it is no longer I who live, but Christ lives in me; and the life which I now live in the flesh I live by faith in the Son of God, who loved me, and delivered Himself up for me."

Chapter 38

Closing Thoughts

Our walk in faith is a life committed to Christ in us. It is a life that submits to the Holy Spirit as the pilot. It is a life that says Christ exalted is more important than self. It is a life of faith in the Life Giver. Jesus said in John 14:6:

> "I am the way, and the truth, and the life; no one comes to the Father, but through me."

Understand that even the Apostle Paul, who wrote most of the New Testament books, said he had not yet arrived but pressed on (Philippians 3:14). If Paul had not yet arrived and he wrote the books we study, then we will not arrive. As Paul did, we too need to press on.

Each day will provide new opportunities for us to grow in our faith in Christ. Each day will provide new opportunities for us to rely on the Spirit of Christ in us to face the battles of the day. The question for us is will our faith be in Christ and His Spirit in us? Or in us? Or in something or someone else? Who will be our pilot?

Only you know in whom or what you have placed your faith. I place my faith in Christ. I trust in His Spirit in my life to make me more like Christ. Each day I believe I get a step closer to the prize. Yes, I sometimes wish I was farther along in God's walk with me, but that is only when I take my eyes off of Jesus and put them on me.

On whom are your eyes? As you take steps today, reflect on putting your eyes on Christ and His walk with you.

Who is your master? Yoke yourself to Jesus and learn from Him.

God walks with us by faith. Faith in the Word of God, both the written, which is the Bible, and the living, which is Jesus Christ. Do you believe and study His word? Do you believe in Christ's finished work? Do you believe in His Spirit in you to work out your salvation? I close with Philippians 2:12, 13:

> "So then, my beloved, just as you have always obeyed, not as in my presence only, but now much more in my absence, work out your salvation with fear and trembling; for it is God who is at work in you, both to will and to work for His good pleasure."

Word of God

"Therefore everyone who hears these word of Mine, and acts upon them, may be compared to a wise man, who built his house upon the rock" (Matthew 7:24).

Chapter 39

Introduction

I have quoted a lot of verses from the Bible, the word of God, to explain the truths that are being presented. Why? Because I believe we know God and know the will of God through His written word. I also believe that the power to save is the word of God.

I actually believe God has communicated Himself in three main ways. We can know God and have faith in God because of His spoken Word, creation, His written Word, the Bible, and His living Word, Jesus Christ. God has made it possible for us to know Him. God wants us to know Him. He wants us to be known by Him.

I find it interesting that the first verse of the Bible begins with our beginning. The first verse of the first book, Genesis 1:1, of the Bible simply says,

> "In the beginning God created the heavens and the earth."

The Bible doesn't start by establishing that God exists. God exists. God has no beginning. The Bible starts with "God created." God through His spoken word created our physical world and us.

As we read the story of creation what we continually read is, "God said" and it happened. Remember when I said we have faith in someone when they can accomplish what they have said. God accomplished everything He said. Genesis 1:3 tells us:

> "Then God said, "Let there be light"; and there was light."

This truth continues throughout creation and history. God speaks and it happens. God spoke through His prophets hundreds of years before events happened. The New Testament is full of Old Testament scriptures prophesizing of Christ's life, death and resurrection. Jesus tells us in Matthew 26:56:

> "But all this has taken place that the Scriptures of the prophets may be fulfilled."

The Bible, the written word of God, records the words, thoughts and actions of God that His Spirit inspired the authors to write. The Bible is often referred to as the scriptures and the inspired Word of God. It contains 66 books written by various authors over hundreds of years. Does it contain everything God did or said? No. John 21:25 tells us:

> "And there are also many other things which Jesus did, which if they were written in detail, I suppose that even the world itself would not contain the books which were written."

The Bible records the word of God that God has chosen to reveal to us. No other book is the Word of God. No other book! It is important to understand that the Bible records what God wants us to know about Him and His plan. It does not tell us everything. And there are no other books written by God. The Bible is the only written word of God.

Do you want to know God? Well, you need to know the word of God. Our knowledge of God comes from Him through His creation, His written word and His living word, Jesus Christ. These next few chapters will primarily address His written word.

Chapter 40

Power

THE WRITTEN WORD OF GOD ACTUALLY HAS A LOT TO SAY ABOUT itself. A verse I quote often is Hebrews 4:12 which reads:

> "For the word of God is living and active and sharper than any two-edged sword, and piercing as far as the division of soul and spirit, of both joints and marrow, and able to judge the thoughts and intentions of the heart."

Hebrews 4:12 is a powerful verse considering everything we have talked about in regards to sin, forgiveness and our hearts. The word of God has a very powerful role in God's walk with us. The word of God judges "the thoughts and intentions of the heart."

This verse tells me that I have to put the word of God in my heart so it will be able to judge me. I like how Psalms 119:9 puts it:

> "How can a young man keep his way pure? By keeping it according to Thy word."

Hebrews 4:12 motivates two questions for me. First, do I meditate on the word of God so that it can judge the thoughts and intentions of my heart? I want God's judgment. Secondly, if God's word is in me and is not judging me, why should I concern myself with the judgment of men? The final authority on my heart is God and His word.

A verse that comforts me is Romans 8:1:

> "There is therefore now no condemnation for those who are in Christ Jesus."

I am very critical of myself. I have had to step back and ask, "Is God condemning me? Is God's word judging me?" If God isn't judging me, there is no reason for me to feel judged.

At the beginning of Christ's ministry, He was tempted by the devil three times. And, each time Jesus responded using the word of God. The temptations are found in Matthew 4:3-10:

> "And the tempter came and said to Him, "If You are the Son of God, command that these stones become bread." But He answered and said, "It is written, 'Man shall not live on bread alone, but on every word that proceeds out of the mouth of the Lord.'" Then the devil took Him into the holy city; and he had Him stand on the pinnacle of the temple, and said to Him, "If You are the Son of God throw Yourself down; for it is written, 'He will give His angels charge concerning You'; and 'On their hands they will bear You up, Lest You strike Your foot against a stone.'" Jesus said to him, "On the other hand, it is written, 'You shall not put the Lord your God to the test.'" Again, the devil took Him to a very high mountain, and showed Him all the kingdoms of the world, and their glory; and he said to Him, "All these things will I give You, if You fall down and worship me." Then Jesus said to him, "Begone, Satan! For it is written, 'You shall worship the Lord your God, and serve Him only.'""

Notice that Christ didn't question whether or not the devil had it right. He responded with the Word of God with His eyes focused on the will of God. He used the word of God correctly. He didn't explain the word of God, He relied on the power of the word of God.

In the second temptation, the devil used the word of God. The difference when the devil used the word of God is that it was for the devil's purposes. When Christ used the word of God it was for God's purposes.

The word of God lets us know the will of God. The word of God keeps us centered in the will of God, if we allow it to judge the thoughts and intentions of our hearts.

Remember Hebrews 12:1, 2:

> "Therefore, since we have so great a cloud of witnesses surrounding us, let us also lay aside every encumbrance, and the sin which so easily entangles us, and let us run with endurance the race that is set before us, fixing our eyes on Jesus, the author and perfecter of faith, who for the joy set before Him endured the cross, despising the shame, and has sat down at the right hand of the throne of God."

Christ stayed focus and used the power of the word of God to resist temptation. That same word of God is available to us. Ephesian 6 which discusses the armor of God tells us in verse 17:

> "...and the sword of the Spirit, which is the word of God."

The word of God is the power of God.

Chapter 41

In Us

PSALMS 119 IS GREAT TO READ WHEN DISCUSSING THE NEED FOR the word of God to be in our hearts.

> Verse 9 - "How can a young man keep his way pure? By keeping it according to Thy word."
>
> Verse 11 - "Thy word I have treasured in my heart, That I may not sin against Thee."
>
> Verse 28 - "My soul weeps because of grief, Strengthen me according to Thy word."
>
> Verses 41-42 - "May Thy lovingkindnesses also come to me, O Lord, Thy salvation according to Thy word; So I shall have an answer for him who reproaches me, For I trust in Thy word."
>
> Verses 71-72 - "It is good for me that I was afflicted, That I may learn Thy statutes. They law of Thy mouth is better to me Than thousands of gold and silver pieces."

You might want to read the whole psalm. I think verse 11 solidifies the need for the word of God in our hearts. If we treasure the word of God in our hearts, it will keep us from sin.

Christ used the word of God in response to the devil's temptation of Him. How much more do we need the word of God to resist temptation? Romans 10:17 says:

> "So faith comes from hearing, and hearing by the word of God."

We need the word of God for our faith. We need to grow in our knowledge of the word of God to grow in faith. Our faith is based on the strength of the word of God in our lives.

In talking about the word of God, we must again look at Christ who is the Word of God. We have no salvation, no hope for our faith, without the finished work of Christ. He was the Word of God come to life. He is our faith.

We must also look at the Holy Spirit when talking about the word of God. The word of God is the sword of the Spirit. The Spirit is at work in us to reveal to us our need for Christ; our need for the word of God.

You cannot believe the word of God and not believe in Christ. And you cannot believe in Christ and not believe the word of God. They are one and the same.

Let's now look at those verses in Psalms 119. We keep our way pure by keeping God's word. We keep ourselves from sin by treasuring God's word in our hearts. God's word strengthens us during times of grief. Our salvation is according to His word.

Verses 41 and 42 tell us to use the word of God just as Christ did when the devil tempted Him. The word of God is our answer.

Verses 71 and 72 are interesting because the Psalmist talks about how affliction drove him to the word of God. He found the word of God better than the riches of the world. Did you know that the riches of the word of God are greater than the riches of the world?

There are so many benefits from knowing the word of God. For me, it helps me focus my eyes on Jesus. Rather than quote the words of men, I quote the beautiful word of God. I find hope and strength in the word of God to face each day.

Chapter 42

Learn

HOW DO YOU GET TO KNOW SOMEONE? YOU SPEND TIME WITH THEM. We get to know God by spending time in His word. We focus our eyes on Jesus by spending time in the word of God. Joshua 1:8 tells us:

> "This book of the law shall not depart from your mouth, but you shall meditate on it day and night, so that you may be careful to do according to all that is written in it; for then you will make your way prosperous, and then you will have success."

I try to spend time reading in the word of God each morning. Right now, I am reading the book of Luke. I read a chapter a day.

At other times, I have picked books of the Bible or passages from the Bible and read them four times a day for a month to let the word of God soak into my heart. That is probably why Romans and Philippians are two of my favorite books, because I did just that with those two books.

There are good devotional books you can read to supplement your Bible reading. You can meditate on the passage your church pastor preached on and let the message seep into your heart.

You can read books like this one alongside your Bible that will help you grow in your understanding

There are a lot of ways to spend time in His word on a personal level. Find what works for you and be prepared to change and grow.

The important thing to remember is to think of spending time in the word of God as spending time with God. Ask Him to help you get to know Him through His word. Ask Him to speak to your heart through His word. Ask Him to securely place His word in your heart.

If you want to know God, you need to spend time in His word. You do not have to read from the beginning to the end, though you can. Think of the Bible as that love letter you just cannot read enough. The word of God is God's love letter to us.

A study Bible can also be quite helpful. I find that study guides for books or biblical topics are helpful. I am an avid reader and so, I read other literature to help me better understand the word of God.

The better we know the word of God, the better we come to know our God and have faith in Him. Consider the word of God as the most important book to read for your success. But always remember that the goal isn't to know the word of God, it is to know the author, our God and Father.

Consider getting involved in a church and a bible study group within the church. God teaches us through others. Others will shed light on a scripture that may answer a question for you or provide you with a deeper answer than you were considering. We learn from each other. Hebrews 10:24, 25 tells us:

> "and let us consider how to stimulate one another to love and good deeds, not forsaking our own assembling together, as is the habit of some, but encouraging one another; and all the more , as you see the day drawing near."

Realize that others need your faith and you need their faith. We are to be in this together. It is through the love and forgiveness we show one another that others will come to know Him. It is an amazing concept.

In choosing a church, you need to consider the doctrine of the church. For me, the main criteria for a church is its position on the finished work of Christ. Unless, the church believes in the sinfulness of man and that the only hope of salvation is Jesus and Jesus alone, I keep looking. Our salvation is the work of the Lord and only the work of the Lord.

There are other things to consider in choosing a church, such as the worship and the programs for the family. You need to find the church where you and your family can worship the Lord together.

You won't agree with everything that is taught and shared in the church. We are individuals with personal relationships with the Lord. We experience Him differently. We experience His walk with us differently.

The important agreement is the finished work of Christ. For the rest you can allow the differences. Differences are okay. Differences challenge us to be sure in our faith. However, if the differences become a hindrance for you, you may consider looking for another church.

Chapter 43

Closing Thoughts

I FIND THAT SPENDING TIME IN THE WORD OF GOD IS SPENDING time with God which settles my heart. I find comfort in His words. I find healing for my heart.

I know what the kind words of a friend does for my emotions. God's word has so much more power. His hugs soothe me and are a reminder of His promises toward me as His child. Matthew 4:4 tells us:

> "But He answered and said, "It is written, 'Man shall not live on bread alone, but on every word that proceeds out of the mouth of God.'""

Remember that this was Christ's response to the devil's temptations. Our spiritual lives need the word of God just as our bodies need bread. When I read verse 11 of the Lord's Prayer found in Matthew 6:9-13:

> "Give us this day our daily bread."

I don't think of physical food, I think of spiritual food. I think of Jesus Christ who is the Word of God. Christ says of Himself in John 6:35:

> "Jesus said to them, 'I am the bread of life; he who comes to Me shall not hunger, and he who believes in Me shall never thirst.'"

Christ is our bread. As I pray this verse, I pray for Christ's presence and His healing power of forgiveness in my live and the lives of others. I ask for God to work in our lives according to His will.

I also think of God's written word as bread for our souls. It is interesting that the verse before is concerned with the will of God being done and the verses after are concerned with forgiveness, temptation and evil. Repeating Psalm 119:11:

> "Thy word I have treasured in my heart, That I may not sin against Thee."

The word of God protects us from sin.

In closing, I caution you to be careful in the Bible you choose. For the word of God you study, you want to choose a Bible that is a literal translation. A paraphrased bible may help you with understanding the word of God but should never be used in lieu of the word of God. The power is in God's word not our interpretation of it.

Psalms 19:7 tells us:

> "The law of the Lord is perfect, restoring the soul; The testimony of the Lord is sure, making wise the simple."

Prayer in Christ

"But you, beloved, building yourselves up on your most holy faith; praying in the Holy Spirit; keep yourselves in the love of God, waiting anxiously for the mercy of our Lord Jesus Christ to eternal life (Jude 1:20, 21)."

Chapter 44

Introduction

PLEASE NOTICE THAT WE ARE DISCUSSING PRAYER IN CHRIST; NOT prayer. There is a difference which I hope to make clear as you read through the chapters that follow.

I want to begin by saying that I believe God answers every prayer we pray and don't pray. I believe He answers every prayer because we have a relationship with Him as our Father. We are His children. What we consider unanswered prayer is us not getting what we requested. Not getting what we requested, is not unanswered prayer. God gives us His answer.

This discussion of prayer is not about how to get what we want from God. This discussion is about how in our relationship to Him in Christ we communicate with Him trusting that His will will be done. It is about communicating with God as He walks with us.

Making requests is part of the communication we have with God. And, I believe He answers every prayer request and I believe He does so by giving us what is best for us. The answer may be no, it may be yes, and it may be wait. All three are answers.

I want to know God will say no when I ask for the wrong thing. I want His protection from my wrong desires. I also want to be able to pour out my heart to my God and know that He hears it all and only responds with what is best for me.

Prayer for me is talking with God. It is telling Him everything that is on my heart and trusting Him with it. It is knowing that my God is in control. It is knowing that I have His grace to endure. It is knowing that I am not alone. It is knowing that He walks with me.

Philippians 4:6, 7 tells us:

> "Be anxious for nothing, but in everything by prayer and supplication with thanksgiving let your requests be made know to God. And the peace of God, which surpasses all comprehension, shall guard your hearts and your minds in Christ Jesus."

Tell God everything and let Him fill you with the peace of the knowledge that He is in control. Notice it says "guard your hearts and minds." The guarding keeps us from sinning by keeping our eyes on Jesus and not placing them on the things for which we are praying.

I like how the verse starts off 'be anxious for nothing." When we are anxious, whatever is causing that anxiety, is interfering with us living. The anxiety becomes our master.

In Philippians 4:6, 7, the Apostle Paul is telling us don't be anxious, instead pray. Let God know what you are feeling and what your needs are and let Him fill you with His peace. Let him guard your heart and mind in Christ.

God is concerned with our hearts and minds. He wants us focused on Him. Prayer lets us take our focus off our circumstances and wants and desires and places it on our relationship with God through Christ Jesus. Prayer puts our hearts and minds in the safest place imaginable. It places them in the center of God's will.

Do I believe God hears my prayer? Yes. Proverbs 15: 29 tells us:

> "But He hears the prayer of the righteous."

I make my requests known to God and ask that His will be done. I use my prayer time to tell God everything that is in my heart, good and bad. I give it to God to manage.

By praying about it, I give it to Him to answer rather than for me to solve. If my request is God's will, it will happen. If it isn't, than I want God's perfect will.

The problem for us is that we don't always like God's answer. It's easy for us to say we want His will, but when we get it, well, we are not so sure. God's perfect will is best.

Chapter 45

What is Prayer

So, I say that God answers prayer. But what is prayer? Is it the actual request? Is it how we make the request? Is it the continual communication with God as we go through the day?

I believe it is actually all three. John 16:23, 23 tell us to ask, in other words, make our request:

> "And in that day you will ask Me no question. Truly, truly, I say to you, if you shall ask the Father for anything, He will give it to you in My name. Until now you have asked for nothing in My name; ask, and you will receive, that your joy may be made full."

What I love about this verse is that it says ask and you will receive. It does not say that I will necessarily receive what I ask for but it does say I will receive. And, it says I will receive so that my joy may be made full. God wants me to have joy.

In Matthew 6:5-9, Jesus tells his disciples how to make their requests known to God; how to pray:

> "And when you pray, you are not to be as the hypocrites; for they love to stand and pray in the synagogues and on the street corners, in order to be seen by men. Truly I say to you, they have their reward in full. But you, when you pray, go into your inner room, and when you have shut your door, pray to your Father who is in secret, and your Father who sees in secret will repay you. And when you are praying, do not use meaningless repetition, as the Gentiles do, for they suppose that they will be heard for their many words. Therefore do not be like them; for your Father knows what you need, before you ask Him. Pray, then, in this way..."

There are several things Jesus tells us about how to pray:

- <u>Go into your inner room</u> - go somewhere private where only God can hear you.
- <u>Do not use meaningless words</u> - pour your heart out. Don't recite prayers as if the power is in the words. The power is with God who wants to answer your prayers. Focus on Him not your prayer.
- <u>Your Father knows what you need before you ask Him</u> - I find such comfort in the fact that God already knows. He knows what we need before we do. We come to Him in prayer not because He needs us to, but because we need to. We need to pour our hearts out to God, so that our focus does not become that which is heavy on our hearts but is on Jesus. Prayer keeps us focused.
- <u>Pray, then, in this way</u> - what follows these words is the Lord's Prayer. I pray that prayer every day now. Why? Because it focusses me on God. It focusses me on His will.

1 Thessalonians 5:16-18 tells us to pray without ceasing:

> "Rejoice always; pray without ceasing; in everything give thanks; for this is God's will for you in Christ Jesus."

This is a beautiful verse. We are to rejoice. We are to pray without ceasing. We are to give thanks in everything. Why? It "is God's will for you in Christ Jesus."

We are to be talking with God throughout our day. We are to be constantly giving our joys, our concerns, and every aspect of our life to God. He cares about the details of our lives. We have a relationship with a loving God who is involved in the details of our lives; He walks with us.

In case you are wondering, yes the Bible does talk about believers praying together. And, I believe all the above applies. My focus here, however, is on the individual prayer life. I believe our relationship with God through prayer begins there.

Chapter 46

Purpose

WHAT DO WE KNOW ABOUT PRAYER? WE KNOW IT'S TELLING GOD what is on our hearts and our minds. We know it's making our requests known to Him. Is it more than that?

I think it is. I think it is about focusing our eyes on Jesus Christ and not on us. I believe it is about putting God's will before our will.

Let's look at the Lord's Prayer found in Matthew 6:9-13:

> "Pray, then in this way:
>
> Our Father who art in heaven,
> Hallowed by Thy name.
> Thy kingdom come. Thy will be done, on earth as it is in heaven.
> Give us this day our daily bread.
> And forgive us our debts, as we also have forgiven our debtors.
> And do not lead us into temptation, but deliver us from evil.

> For thing is the kingdom, and the power, and the glory,
> forever.
> Amen.

I am not going to say a lot on the Lord's Prayer. There are really good books to read on this subject. I just want to point out what the Lord has been teaching me as I pray through the Lord's Prayer.

<u>Our Father who art in heaven</u> - God exists and wants us to know Him as a Father. We have a personal relationship with our God. Where is He? He is not confined by our physical world. He is in heaven.

I am glad He is not confined by our world. He is able to do all that He promises. Nothing in this world can interfere with the will of God for my life.

<u>Hallowed by Thy name</u> - God is holy. That Jesus uses God's holiness rather than another attribute is fitting. It is a reminder that God is not like us. He truly can do all that He says He will do. The gospel message is that we are sinners and through Christ we have forgiveness.

<u>Thy kingdom come, Thy will be done, on earth as it is in heaven</u> - Two quick thoughts: God's kingdom will come. As Christians, we should want the kingdom of God over this world. Our homes are with Him.

The heart of every prayer should be that God's will be done here on earth. The will of God needs to be central to the life of a Christian. Are we wanting our will or the will of God? In our relationships with the Lord, our desire should always be the will of God. It is a lifelong prayer process to develop this kind of relationship but well worth it.

<u>Give us this day our daily bread</u> – Jesus tells us in John 6:35 that He is the bread of life:

> "Jesus said to them, "I am the bread of life; he who comes to Me shall not hunger....""

Jesus also says in Matthew 26:26:

> "And while they were eating, Jesus took some bread, and after a blessing, He broke it and gave it to the disciples, and said, "Take, eat; this is My body.""

Christ is our daily bread. What we all need is a closer walk with Him. Each day we need to renew ourselves in His love. It is in Christ that we can make our requests known to God the Father and He will accomplish His will concerning us.

God is most concerned with our relationship with Him. We, too, should be most concerned with our relationship with Him. Prayer helps us focus on Him.

Still, it is amazing to think that God hears us and cares about us. He wants to take care of us. He wants to answer our requests.

<u>And forgive us our debts; as we also have forgiven our debtors</u> - Forgiveness. Please review the chapters on forgiveness. It is a necessary part of our relationship with God and each other.

<u>And do not lead us into temptation, but deliver us from evil</u> - I would like to write a book on this verse. All of us are capable of all imaginable sins. Only by the grace of God do we not commit them. Oh how we need to pray that God deliver us from the evil of sin.

What a powerful prayer. What a wonderful example of how to pray. I pray this prayer daily because it expresses the desires of my heart before God.

We need God involved in our lives. We need to see prayer as a way to develop our relationship with the Lord rather than a way to get what we want.

Prayer is us having God get involved in our lives and the lives of others. It is asking God to work in our hearts and minds. And yes, it is also making our requests known to God. However, first and foremost, prayer is about developing our love relationship with the Lord; developing His walk with us.

In the next few chapters I will be specifically talking about the ways God answers prayer requests. As you read these chapters, please be mindful that at all times I have in view that it is God's walk with us, first and foremost, that is our purpose for prayer.

Chapter 47

God Answers Yes

THE BIBLE IS FULL OF ANSWERED PRAYERS WITH GOD GIVING THE person that for which they prayed. However, God doesn't give to His people because He is obligated by something in us. He does not owe us anything. He answers yes because it is according to His perfect will for us.

I want to look at a prayer in scripture that I believe points to the relationship we have in God when it comes to prayer rather than the request itself. 2 Kings 18:1 - 20:21 tells the story of King Hezekiah. Within that story is a specific passage about God working in Hezekiah's life and prayer. Let's begin in 2 Kings 20:1-5:

> "In those days Hezekiah became mortally ill. And Isaiah the prophet the son of Amoz, came to him and said to him, "Thus says the Lord, 'Set your house in order, for you shall die and not live.'" Then he turned his face to the wall, and prayed to the Lord, saying "Remember now, O Lord, I beseech Thee, how I have walked before Thee in truth and with a whole heart, and have done what is good in Thy sight." And Hezekiah

> wept bitterly. And it came about before Isaiah had gone out of the middle court, that the word of the Lord came to him, saying, "Return and say to Hezekiah the leader of My people, 'Thus says the Lord, the God of your father David, "I have heard your prayer, I have seen your tears; behold, I will heal you."'""

Hezekiah poured his heart out to God. And what was God's message - "I have heard your prayer, I have seen your tears; behold I will heal you." Now, please note, Hezekiah asked God to remember him and remember his relationship with God; he did not ask for healing. Hezekiah's prayer request was about His relationship with God. God's answer was that He would heal him.

God knew the desires of Hezekiah's heart without it being said. Hezekiah trusted his relationship with God such that He knew God would know. 2 Kings 18:5 gives us a snapshot of Hezekiah's relationship with God:

> "He trusted in the Lord, the God of Israel; so that after him there was none like him among all the kings of Judah, nor among those who were before him."

It was that kind of relationship that Hezekiah called upon. And, God answered. God heard the unspoken words as well as the spoken. Hezekiah was not ready to die. I think of what the Apostle Paul said in Philippians 1:21-25:

> "For to me, to live is Christ, and to die is gain. But if I am to live on in the flesh, this will mean fruitful labor for me; and I do not know which to choose. But I am hard-pressed from both directions, having the desire to depart and be with Christ, for that is very much better; yet to remain on in the flesh is more necessary for your sake. And convinced of this, I know that I shall remain

> and continue with you all for your progress and joy in the faith.

Paul felt that he had more to do for God. Hezekiah felt he had more he wanted to do. I cannot fully understand what God was doing but I don't believe it was ever His intention that Hezekiah die at that moment.

Why God gave Isaiah the message to tell Hezekiah he would die, I do not know. But I do believe the message was meant for the moment. And since we are looking at this closely I want to continue to the next yes answer to prayer Hezekiah gets.

In verse 7 (2 Kings 20:7) we are told that Hezekiah recovered. And yet, in verse 8 we have Hezekiah asking:

> "Now Hezekiah said to Isaiah, "What will be the sign that the Lord will heal me, and that I shall go up to the house of the Lord the third day?""

Isaiah gives him the sign. I think it is actually quite bold of Hezekiah to ask for a sign especially after he had just been healed and he only had to wait three days. But God answered his request. Maybe bold in prayer is good. And oh, to have the relationship with God that Hezekiah had to claim in prayer.

I have two more thoughts on God's answer to his prayer:

Notice that Hezekiah was promised he would go to the house of the Lord on the third day. In other words, he would rise up out of bed from his illness on the third day. Isn't that what Christ did; he rose on the third day? I find that interesting.

Also, God promised him 15 more years of life (2 Kings 20:6). After Hezekiah dies we read in 2 Kings 21:1:

> "Manasseh was twelve years old when he became king...."

After I do the math, Manasseh was born three years after the prayer. Hezekiah was not done with what he had to do.

God said yes to Hezekiah. I do believe it always was God's will that Hezekiah live 15 more years and that this prayer has a message for us. Look at how Hezekiah's prayer was dependent on his walk with God, "in truth and with a whole heart."

God looks at the heart of a person as he listens to the prayer. As I said, I pour out my heart before the Lord trusting Him for what is best. Jesus tells us in John 14:13-14:

> "And whatever you ask in My name, that will I do, that the Father may be glorified in the Son. If you ask Me anything in My name, I will do it."

Christ is telling us that if we ask anything in His name He will do it. Does that mean we tack His name at the end of our prayer? No. It means that we are asking with Christ in control of our lives, our hearts and our prayers. And how did Christ pray In Matthew 26:42:

> "Thy will be done."

Christ prefaces the Lord's Prayer with the following words in Matthew 6:8:

> "Therefore do not be like them; for your Father knows what you need, before you ask Him."

Who was them? The hypocrites and gentiles who trusted more in their prayer than in their God. It was more about their request than a relationship with God in Christ. Our prayer life needs to result from a right relationship with God.

Chapter 48

God Answers No

We don't like the answer no. However, isn't it a common answer we give when someone asks us to do something we know we should not do? I think the first word a baby learns is no.

I believe for God's yes to be yes, He needs to say no. God telling me no, tells me God is going to give me His best, not what I think is best. God might tell me His reason and He might not.

I believe His no to my request is a yes to His will being done, which is the more important answer to my prayer. His no also tells me that He is committed to a relationship where I can trust His best and He is in control; rather than a relationship where I am in control.

God said no to King David. David had built a house for himself and wanted to build a house for the Lord. The story unfolds in 2 Samuel 7:1-13:

> "Now it came about when the king lived in his house, and the Lord had given him rest on every side from all his enemies, that the king said to Nathan the prophet, "See now, I dwell in a house of cedar, but the ark of God dwells within tent curtains." And Nathan said to

> the king, "Go, do all that is in your mind, for the Lord is with you." But it came about in the same night that the word of the Lord came to Nathan, saying, "Go and say to My servant David, 'Thus says the Lord, "Are you the one who should build Me a house to dwell in?... When you days are complete and you lie down with your fathers, I will raise up your descendant after you, who will come forth from you, and I will establish his kingdom. He shall build a house for My name, and I will establish the throne of his kingdom forever.'""

Did David ask for something wrong? No. God just had a different plan in mind. A house would be built for God's name, David just would not be the one to build it. This passage doesn't tell us why God said no to David, only that He did.

King Solomon, however, in 1 Kings 8:17, 18 does tell us this:

> "Now it was in the heart of my father David to build a house for the name of the Lord, the God of Israel. But the Lord said to my father David, 'Because it was in your heart to build a house for My name, you did well that it was in your heart.'"

God did not say no to David because of David's sin or because he asked the wrong thing. David is told that he 'did well that it was in your heart.' God said no because He had His perfect plan.

God also said no to the Apostle Paul. Let's read 2 Corinthians 12:7-9:

> "And because of the surpassing greatness of the revelations, for this reason, to keep me from exalting myself, there was given me a thorn in the flesh, a messenger of Satan to buffet me - to keep me from exalting myself! Concerning this I entreated the Lord three times that it might depart from me. And He has

> said to me, 'My grace is sufficient for you, for power is perfected in weakness.' Most gladly, therefore, I will rather boast about my weaknesses, that the power of Christ may dwell in me."

The Apostle Paul tells us that he has a thorn in the flesh and that he asked God to remove it. I think Paul did not tell us what the thorn was because the request is not what is important; the answer is what is important.

God told Paul that His grace was sufficient. God told Paul that His power was perfected in Paul's weakness. And Paul gladly accepted the answer.

Paul could accept the no because His relationship with God through Christ was more important than him getting his request. Paul let God know what He wanted. God gave Paul His answer. And Paul put the answer into the perspective that Christ in Him was far more important than anything else in his life.

I believe the prayer is shared with us to put our prayer requests in perspective. Where is your focus? Is your focus on your prayer request or on God? Paul would gladly rather have the power of Christ in his weakness than have the weakness removed. His relationship with Christ was more valuable.

In your prayers, are you seeking God to work in your life or are you seeking your request? I give my requests to God, but I am seeking Him not my requests. I want God actively involved in my life accomplishing what is best for me. I want God actively accomplishing His best in the lives of others.

God always has a good reason when He answers no.

Chapter 49

God Answers Wait

I THINK WAIT IS PROBABLY THE HARDEST ANSWER TO ACCEPT. AT least with no we have an answer. Wait means you have to be patient until the proper time. Wait is an answer in God's world.

When I think of waiting for an answer to prayer, I always think of Joseph. He was the favorite son of Israel. God had given him dreams of grandeur. But the path to the grandeur was less than pleasant.

We have discussed him in earlier chapters. His brothers sell him into slavery. His master's wife tries to seduce him and he ends up in prison. Joseph is still in prison when we pick up the story in Genesis 40:14-41:1:

> "Only keep me in mind when it goes well with you, and please do me a kindness by mentioning me to Pharaoh, and get me out of this house…Yet the chief cupbearer did not remember Joseph, but forgot him. Now it happened at the end of two full years…"

Joseph, expecting to be released in two days, waited in prison to be remembered for two full years. I have to believe two years in prison felt longer than two years. And how did Joseph view this time? Look with me at Genesis 45:4-8:

> "Then Joseph said to his brothers, "Please come closer to me." And they came closer. And he said, "I am your brother Joseph, whom you sold into Egypt. And now do not be grieved or angry with yourselves, because you sold me here; for God sent me before you to preserve life. For the famine has been in the land these two years, and there are still five years in which there will be neither plowing nor harvesting. And God sent me before you to preserve for you a remnant in the earth, and to keep you alive by a great deliverance. Now, therefore, it was not you who sent me here, but God..."

Joseph saw God's plan in the wait. He saw God's plan in the circumstances. Joseph knew God was with him working out His plan for Joseph's life. Joseph understood God's perfect will for him. He had a strong relationship with his God.

Another interesting wait answer to prayer involves Martha, Mary, Lazarus and Jesus. The story is told in John 11:1-44:

> Now a certain man was sick, Lazarus of Bethany, the village of Mary and her sister Martha...The sisters therefore sent to Him saying, "Lord, behold, he whom You love is sick." But when Jesus heard it, He said, "This sickness is not unto death; but for the glory of God, that the Son of God may be glorified by it." Now Jesus loved Martha, and her sister, and Lazarus. When therefore He heard that he was sick, He stayed then two days longer in the place where He was...after that He said to them, "Our friend Lazarus has fallen asleep; but I go, that I may awaken him out of sleep." The disciples therefore said to Him, "Lord, if he has fallen asleep, he will recover."...Then Jesus therefore said to them

> plainly, "Lazarus is dead, and I am glad for your sakes that I was not there, so that you may believe; but let us go to him." ...Martha therefore said to Jesus, "Lord, if You had been here, my brother would not have died. Even now I know that whatever You ask of God, God will give You"...Therefore, when Mary came where Jesus was, she saw Him, and fell at His feet, saying to Him, "Lord, if You had been here, my brother would not have died."...And so they removed the stone. And Jesus raised His eyes, and said, "Father, I thank Thee that Thou heardest Me. And I knew that Thou hearest Me always; but because of the people standing around I said it, that they may believe that Thou didst send me." And when He has said these things, He cried out with a loud voice, "Lazarus, come forth." He who had died came forth..."

Christ purposefully waited to answer Martha's and Mary's request to come and heal their brother. Both Martha and Mary knew that Lazarus would still be alive if Jesus had just come. God had a bigger plan and so they had to wait.

Martha, Mary and Lazarus had very strong relationships with Jesus. They trusted Him and knew He could do what they requested. However, they did not understand why He didn't do it as they requested. And I believe this is key, while they understood how they wanted Jesus to answer their request, they did not understand that God had a better way.

I believe God chose these three for this story because of their relationship with Jesus. I also believe He answered it the way He did to remind all of us that His way of answering our requests are best. They got what they requested just not their way.

Wait is an answer to prayer. Wait means God has a bigger purpose than our request and we need to have faith in Him. God's plan is more important than our plan. We need to trust His walk with us.

Chapter 50
Thanksgiving

I WAS FORTUNATE ENOUGH TO MINSTER IN GREECE FOR TWO YEARS and learn the language. One of the things I learned is that the root word in the Greek word for thanksgiving is the Greek word for grace. Thanksgiving is found in grace.

Let's look at Philippians 4:6 again:

> "Be anxious for nothing, but in everything by prayer and supplication with thanksgiving..."

And again what did Paul learn in 2 Corinthians 12:9:

> "And He has said to me, "My grace is sufficient for you, for power is perfected in weakness.""

We pray with thanksgiving because we have the grace of God in our lives. Ephesians 2:8 tell us:

> "For by grace you have been saved through faith; and not of yourselves, it is the gift of God."

We have the grace of God; what more do we need? We have God's unconditional love, unconditional acceptance, and the healing power of His forgiveness. His Spirit is ever present in our lives to give us power to live for Him. He walks with us. Is not all that sufficient to give thanks?

We give thanks because of all that we do have in Christ. We give thanks because God will only do good in regards to those things for which we pray. Our thanksgiving expresses our faith in a holy and righteous God who loves us.

When I get a good parking spot, I say thank you. When I don't get a good parking spot, I tell the Lord thank you because I know He has a reason. We need to give thanks in all things because it keeps our focus on Him and not on us or our circumstances.

And, if for no other reason, we give thanks because of the grace of God in our lives beginning with our salvation. Have you ever stopped and just started thanking the Lord for all the good in your life? It is an amazing experience.

Chapter 51

Closing Thoughts

GOD WANTS OUR HONESTY. GOD CAN HANDLE OUR RAW EMOTION. God wants what is best for us. We often do not know how to pray so He has given us the spirit of God who prays for us. Romans 8:26, 27 tell us:

> "And in the same way the Spirit also helps our weakness; for we do not know how to pray as we should, but the Spirit Himself intercedes for us with groanings too deep for words; and He who searches the hearts knows what the mind of the Spirit is, because He intercedes for the saints according the will of God."

The key is that "He intercedes according to the will of God." Isn't that what we really want? I know I really want the will of God. Yes, I sometimes wish His will was different. But that wish is in the moment. When I take my eyes off of the moment and fix them on Jesus, I only want the will of God. God's walk with me is more important than my request.

Christ in John 14:14 said:

> "If you ask Me anything in My name, I will do it."

When you think about what it means to ask in His name, let us look at how He prayed in the Garden of Gethsemane just before His crucifixion. The first prayer is found in Matthew 26:39:

> "My Father, if it is possible, let this cup pass from Me;
> yet not as I will, but as Thou wilt."

The second prayer is found in Matthew 26:42:

> "My Father, if this cannot pass away unless I drink it,
> Thy will be done."

I want you to notice that in both prayers Christ asked that the will of the Father be done. When we pray in His name it is with the understanding that the will of the Father is to be done.

I also want you to notice a change in the prayer. There was a change in Christ's praying from the first prayer to the second. I believe the change in the second prayer was the Father answering the first prayer. Christ's relationship with His Father was influencing His prayer.

Often the things we pray for are more about what we want rather than wanting God's will for us. Christ showed raw emotion in His prayer and, more importantly, the desire for the will of God to ultimately be done.

Christ knew He would go to the cross. He knew the will of His Father. But He still prayed.

Are you honest in your prayer life with the Lord?

Do you see God as someone to give you what you want or someone to Whom you submit your will?

Are you more concerned with getting what you want or the will of God?

Do you thank God for all that He has already given you in Christ?

Do you allow your relationship with your Father to influence your prayer life?

We serve a great God who spared not His own Son that we might have life. How could His will for us not be best for us?

1 John 5:14, 15 tells us:

> "And this is the confidence which we have before Him, that, if we ask anything according to His will, He hears us. And if we know that He hears us in whatever we ask, we know that we have the requests which we have asked from Him."

Who We are in Christ

"Trust in the Lord with all your heart, and do not lean on your own understanding. In all your ways acknowledge Him, and He will make your paths straight (Proverbs 3:5, 6)."

Chapter 52

Introduction

I BELIEVE UNDERSTANDING WHO WE ARE IN CHRIST IS IMPORTANT. I believe that understanding who we are in Christ helps define us and keeps our eyes focused on God. We are lost until we understand that our true sense of self is only found in our identification with Christ. It is only found in His walk with us that we are complete.

A human psychological theme is about building one's self-esteem. Well, as Christians, I do not think that building our self-esteem should be our theme. I do not believe that it is God's theme for us. I believe God's theme is to build our "in Christ' esteem; to keep our eyes focused on Christ.

In horse racing, the horses wear blinkers (I just looked up the name). The purpose of the blinkers is to keep the horse's eyes on the race in front of him and not look back. Seeing ourselves 'in Christ' are the blinkers to focus us on the race we have as Christians.

God does not want to build us up in ourselves; that would be looking back. He wants to build us up in Christ; that is looking forward. 'In Christ' is the critical difference between God psychology and human psychology.

On whom are your eyes focused? On yourself or on Christ? On whom do you want them focused? Who defines your sense of self? You? Others? Christ? I want Christ to define me. I want His walk with me to define me.

Remember what the Apostle Paul tells us in Galatians 2:20:

> "I have been crucified with Christ; and it is no longer I who live, but Christ lives in me; and the life which I now live in the flesh I live by faith in the Son of God, who loved me, and delivered Himself up for me."

Paul says he no longer lives but was crucified with Christ. It is now Christ who lives in Him. The life he now lives is by faith in Christ. His eyes are on Christ.

Philippians 3:3-9 is another a good passage:

> "for we are the true circumcision, who worship in the Spirit of God and glory in Christ Jesus and put no confidence in the flesh, although I myself might have confidence even in the flesh, if anyone else has a mind to put confidence in the flesh, I far more: circumcised the eighth day, of the nation of Israel, of the tribe of Benjamin, a Hebrew of Hebrew; as to the Law a Pharisee; as to zeal, a persecutor of the church; as to the righteousness which is in the Law, found blameless. But whatever things were gain to me, those things I have counted as loss for the sake of Christ. More than that, I count all things to be loss in view of the surpassing value of knowing Christ Jesus my Lord, for whom I have suffered the loss of all things, and count them but rubbish in order that I may gain Christ, and may be found in Him, not having a righteousness of my own derived from the Law, but that which is through faith in Christ, the righteousness which comes from God on the basis of faith."

Paul had very positive self-esteem but considered his self-esteem loss in view of the esteem he would have in Christ through faith. Who he was in Christ was gain over who he was in self. To Paul, any worth he had in the world was nothing compared to the worth he had in Christ.

Chapter 53

The Problem With "I"

The problem with "I" is that "I" likes to have control. "I likes to take the credit." "I" likes to be god in our lives.

I actually tried a little experiment. I tried to communicate without "I" being in my vocabulary. I failed miserably. But what I did realize is that "I" only gets power if I truly believe in "I." If I know all that I am is because of whom I am in Christ, than "I" does not have power over me.

Remember the struggle in Romans 7. It was between the sinful flesh, "I", and the spiritual self who was in Christ. Paul tells us that in our life of faith, "I" no longer lives but Christ lives in me.

The reason I tried the experiment was that I was thinking about how we talk about a team's downfall or an individual's downfall being a result of them starting to believe their own propaganda. Well, I thought of all the times we say "I" and realized that it is like our own propaganda.

I heard a minister once talk about everything he had done for Christ. And I was sitting there thinking, you did what? Where was God in all that you did? He never once mentioned God's power.

I believe we should talk about how God uses us to encourage one another. But he wasn't talking about how God was using him. He was talking about all that he had done. And then he asked, if we were doing anything. I was thinking that no "I" have not done anything for the Lord.

"I" cannot accomplish anything. Christ in me can accomplish all things. By not saying "I," I was trying to figure out how to get "I" out and Christ in. I was trying to put blinkers on.

I wanted my eyes off of me and on Christ in me. I wanted to acknowledge that it was in Christ that I was special in God's eyes. It is in Christ that I accomplish all that the Lord has given me to do.

I believe that what happened to Adam and Eve when they sinned is that they stopped looking at who they were in their relationship to God. Genesis 3:6 tells us:

> "When the woman saw that the tree was good for food, and that it was a delight to the eyes, and that the tree was desirable to make one wise, she took from its fruit and ate; and she gave also to her husband with her, and he ate."

Notice that the tree was a delight to her eyes and then the tree was desirable and then she took the fruit and ate. Her eyes shifted from being delighted in the Lord to being delighted in the tree.

The tree went from being good for food to making her wise. Her eyes shifted from God and His word to the tree and her desires. Her eyes went from the will of God to the will of self and she sinned. And Adam, did the same. We do the same.

If we return to Romans 7 it tells us in verse 18:

> "For I know that nothing good dwells in me, that it, in my flesh; for the wishing is present in me, but the doing of the good is not."

In man's psychology, there is good in all men. In God's psychology, "nothing good dwells in me." Romans 3:23 tell us:

> "for all have sinned, and fall short of the glory of God."

"I" is a sinner. "I" falls short of the glory of God. "I" is striving for the glory of men not for the glory of God.

Luke 16:13 tells us:

> "No servant can serve two masters; for either he will hate the one, and love the other, or else he will hold to one, and despise the other. You cannot serve God and mammon."

The point I want to make with this verse is that you cannot serve "I" and God. You cannot have two pilots in your life. Do you want to build up self? Or, do you want to build up self in Christ?

The Apostle Paul tells us in 2 Corinthians 10:18:

> "For not he who commends himself is approved, but whom the Lord commends."

Building up our self-esteem does nothing for our approval before God. We may feel better about ourselves, others may applaud us, but we gain nothing in our relationship with the Lord. The Lord commends us in Christ.

"I" keeps us from a relationship with the Lord. "I" is about our relationship with self who becomes our god. We need to focus on who we are in Christ and our relationship with our God, the one and only true God.

Chapter 54

In Christ Esteem

The word of God says a lot about who we are in Christ. In Christ, we are forgiven; I John 2:12:

> "I am writing to you, little children, because your sins are forgiven you for His name's sake."

In Christ, we are holy and beloved; Colossians 3:12:

> "And so, as those who have been chosen of God, holy and beloved."

In Christ, we are righteous; Philippians 3:9:

> "and may be found in Him, not having a righteousness of my own derived from the Law, but that which is through faith in Christ, the righteousness which comes from God on the basis of faith."

In Christ, we are saints; 1 Corinthians 1:2:

> "to the church of God which is at Corinth, to those who have been sanctified in Christ Jesus, saints by calling, with all who in every place call upon the name of our Lord Jesus Christ, their Lord and ours."

In Christ, the list continues. Who we are in Christ is so much better than who we are in self. Who we are in Christ is pleasing to the Lord. Hebrews 13:20, 21 tells us:

> "Now, the God of peace, who brought up from the dead the great Shepherd of the sheep through the blood of the eternal covenant, even Jesus our Lord, equip you in every good thing, to do His will, working in us that which is pleasing in His sight, through Jesus Christ, to whom be the glory forever and ever."

I believe it is a fine line we walk when we seek to encourage one another and it requires balance. God wants to heal us of the hurts and the damage done by the words and actions of others. However, he wants to heal us through His relationship with us in Christ. We sometimes forget that and try to build one another up in our 'self' qualities.

God, as our pilot, will use our self-qualities. He uses those self-qualities in Christ. They become in Christ qualities. In Christ, the qualities are made perfect.

Faith, the Word of God and prayer give us that balance in our own lives and balance when seeking to encourage others. They give us the skills to help others to develop their in Christ esteem. John 15:5 tells us:

> "I am the vine, you are the branches; he who abides in Me, and I in him, he bears much fruit, for apart from Me you can do nothing."

We build our in Christ esteem by knowing and listening to what God says about us. In Christ, we are complete. In Christ, we are the best we can ever be. In Christ, we are pleasing to God.

God uses forgiveness to heal the brokenness in our sense of self and uses His love to build us up in Christ. Our Father cares about our development as His children. He wants us to know the fullness of His love toward us.

Remember, we are the airplane and He is the pilot. He is also the mechanic. He understands how we are put together and the maintenance we need to perform at our best under His control.

I make a habit of claiming who I am in Christ. For example, take the verses above and say the following:

I John 1:12 - Thank You, Father, that in Christ Jesus my sins are forgiven for His name's sake.

Colossians 3:12 - Thank You, Father, that in Christ Jesus I am Your chosen, holy and beloved.

Philippians 3:9 - Thank You, Father, that in Christ Jesus I may be found in Him, not having a righteousness of my own, but that which is through faith in Christ, the righteousness which comes from You.

1 Corinthians 1:2 - Thank You, Father, that in Christ Jesus I am sanctified, a saint by calling.

I have a list of verses that I keep at my bedside. And when I feel especially down about who I am, I pray them through. The knowledge of who I am in Christ fills me with worth and value; fills me with unconditional acceptance.

Isn't that what we are seeking anyway? A sense of worth, a sense of value, and a sense that we are acceptable. We have God's unconditional acceptance of us in Christ. What greater acceptance is there?

Chapter 55

Closing Thoughts

MAN'S PSYCHOLOGY SOUNDS GOOD. AND, IF SOMEONE DOES NOT have God, it is really their only hope for a sense of self. But we, in Christ, have God the Father to hope in. We, in Christ, have the Holy Spirit to hope in. We, in Christ, have everything we need for self to hope in.

Who will define you? Will you? Will others? Will man's psychology? Will God?

Do you need healing? God heals. Jesus tells us in Luke 5:31, 32:

> "And Jesus answered and said to them, "It is not those who are well who need a physician, but those who are sick. I have not come to call the righteous but sinners to repentance.""

Jesus said this verse in response to the religious leaders complaining that He was eating with sinners. Jesus tells us that He came to heal sinners with His power of forgiveness. His forgiveness heals.

Our sin and the sin of others against us does distort our sense of self. Through the healing power of Christ's forgiveness that distortion can be healed.

His forgiveness returns to us what was lost in the garden. What did Adam say in Genesis 3:10?

> "And he said, "I heard the sound of Thee in the garden, and I was afraid because I was naked; so I hid myself.""

In Christ, we do not need to hide ourselves from God. When Christ died we are told in Matthew 27:51:

> "And behold, the veil of the temple was torn in two from top to bottom."

The tearing of the veil is significant. The veil separated the Holy of Holies from the rest of the temple. Only the high priest could enter on behalf of himself and the people. No one else could enter.

However, by the veil being torn, God is saying to us that we may now enter into His presence through Jesus Christ. In Christ, there is not a veil that separates us from our God. We do not have to be afraid, because we are clothed in Christ.

I would much rather have a sense of self in Christ than any other person, including myself. He died on the Christ for me, what greater gift can someone give?

Are you allowing yourself to be built up in Christ? Or, are you looking to other people or things to build you up?

Yes, we need other people. I need other people. But, I want God, in Christ, to define me. I want God, in Christ, to be my sense of self.

Who defines you?

Who gives you a sense of who you are?

On whom are your eyes for your sense of self?

I choose Christ. I chose to build up self in Christ. Psalms 139:14 tells me, tells us:

> "I will give thanks to Thee for I am fearfully and wonderfully made; Wonderful are Thy works, and my soul knows it very well."

Chapter 56

He Walks with Us

Yes, I purposely called this chapter by the same title as the first chapter. I want to finish that chapter now that you understand the truths that anchor God's walk with me.

I think of God's walk with us like hiking a mountain range. There will be peaks, there will be valleys, and there will be mesas. We will have our victories, we will have our sorrows, and we will have time of rest. And always, God will be with us.

Victories can take many forms. It could be new insight into one of God's truths. It could be that special answered prayer. It could be the new way you handle an old situation. I believe challenges to our faith lead to victories. Victories come from climbing to peaks in our faith.

When I think of victory in faith I think of the Apostle Peter. Peter denied His Lord three times prior to the crucifixion. Later, after the power of the Holy Spirit has come upon him, he speaks boldly to the same religious leaders who had Christ crucified. This is what the leaders said about Peter in Acts 4:13:

> "Now as they observed the confidence of Peter and John, and understood that they were uneducated and untrained men, they were marveling, and began to recognize them as having been with Jesus."

I daresay for Peter that that was a victory in God's walk with him. Peter does go on to die for his faith.

Sorrows are plentiful in this world of sin. Sorrows test our faith. There are no easy answers for the pains we endure. For me, the book of Job is about faith through sorrow. There often is no explanation for our sorrow, but there is God holding our hands and walking with us through the sorrow.

The valleys will come. My deepest moments in my relationship with God the Father are in the valleys. Christ understands sorrow. Isaiah 53:3 tells us:

> "He was despised and forsaken of men, A man of sorrows, and acquainted with grief; And like one from whom men hide their face, He was despised, and we did not esteem Him."

And, of course, the mesas. The time when we rest and allow our spirits to absorb the latest victory or sorrow. Elijah is a great example of God caring for us when we need to rest. The story takes place in 1 Kings 18:1 – 19:18. I encourage you to read it.

It is okay for us to need to rest. I think of the sabbath day. God knows we need rest. Jesus tells us in Matthew 11:28:

> "Come to Me, all who are weary and heavy-laden, and I will give you rest."

As God walks with you, be prepared for the victories and the sorrows and the times of rest. Enjoy Him as He walks with you through the challenges of each. Hold onto His hand and His truths as He walks with you. And remember Christ's final words to us in Matthew 28:20:

> "and lo, I am with you always, even to the end of the age."

Final Thoughts

A lot has been shared on these pages. Step by step God walks with us storing these truths in our hearts.

Where do we go from here? We trust God to build our faith, to give us hearts to forgive, to make us prayer warriors, and above all else, keep our eyes focused on Him.

God walks with us by faith; faith in God's word, faith in God's promises, faith in God's power. The Holy Spirit is with us each step of the way. We will stumble and sometimes fall, but God and His word are ever faithful. He will continue to walk with us. As the apostle Paul said, we need to press on.

I encourage you to find a group of people who you can trust to hold you up. I always think of the story in Exodus 17:8-12:

> "Then Amalek came and fought against Israel at Rehpidim. So Moses said to Joshua, "Choose men for us, and go out fight against Amalek. Tomorrow I will station myself on the top of the hill with the staff of God in my hand." And Joshua did as Moses told him, and fought against Amalek; and Moses, Aaron, and Hur went up to the top of the hill. So it came about when Moses held his hand up, that Israel prevailed, and when he let his hand down, Amalek prevailed. But

> Moses' hands were heavy. Then they took a tone and put it under him, and he sat on it; and Aaron and Hur supported his hands, one on one side and one on the other. Thus his hands were steady until the sun set. So Joshua overwhelmed Amalek and his people with the edge of the sword."

The people in battle needed Moses to be faithful in his role to succeed. But note, Moses also needed others to help him succeed in his role. We need each other to face the battles we will face. Find people who can support you as God fulfills His purpose for your life.

And remember, He walks with you!

I close with Romans 16:25-27:

> "Now to Him who is able to establish you according to my gospel and the preaching of Jesus Christ, according to the revelation of the mystery which has been kept secret for long ages past, but now is manifested, and by the Scriptures of the prophets, according to the commandment of the eternal God, has been made known to all the nations, leading to obedience of faith; to the only wise God, through Jesus Christ, be the glory forever. Amen."

About the Author

MARY WAS A SENIOR IN COLLEGE WHEN SHE COMMITTED HER LIFE to the Lord. Upon graduation, rather than pursue her engineering career, she became a missionary. Often she was asked why she gave up the money and the opportunities offered her as a woman engineer.

Her response was always that she did not give up anything. If God wanted her to be an engineer again one day, she would be. Well, some twenty years later she was getting her Master's Degree in Engineering Management and her Professional Engineering License in Mechanical Engineering. Earlier she had received her Master's Degree in Counseling.

Mary would say the path she followed is the one God planned for her and that He has walked with her the whole way. One of her favorite comments is from *The Hiding Place* by Corrie Ten Boom – There are no ifs in the will of God.

She is retired now and is focusing on writing and ministry. She lives with family in Sacramento, CA.

Contact information:
Mlyon2004@gmail.com

11858727R00124

Made in the USA
San Bernardino, CA
30 May 2014